23

The GOAT Case For

LeBron James

Published by Vellum Owl LLC

ISBN: 979-8-9985346-1-4

Copyright © 2025 Vellum Owl LLC

First Paperback Edition, May 2025

Published in the United States of America

23

Table of Contents

Author's Note

    Due to the fact that any discussion of a sportsman's legacy will deal in large part with statistical data, the pages of this book will hold perhaps an unusually amount of numbers. In order to help distinguish one category of numbers from another and avoid a finished look more akin to that of a mathematical textbook, numbers which deal primarily with everyday descriptions such as age or otherwise modify nouns in the mode of an adjective will often be written out linguistically. On the other hand, numbers which represent statistical information or otherwise refer specifically to modifiers of nouns related to one's basketball resumé (such as, "In year 7 of his career...") will be represented through their Arabic numerals.

    This is a book comparing the basketball careers of two men: LeBron James and Michael Jordan. Should LeBron choose to continue his NBA profession for another few years, readers may understandably have a degree of puzzlement about this book's 2025 release date. If we are going to write up a comparison of the two careers, why not wait until the cement is dry for both of them? The answer has to do with a question of longevity and how we should value it in sports. The longer LeBron continues to play, the higher his stat totals will rise and the larger the gap between him and Michael Jordan will grow on those fronts. This will likely have the dual consequences of inspiring a braggadocious fervor on the part of LeBron's proponents while also inspiring a reactionary, defensive dismissal of such statistical categories on the part of Jordan fans. The more different the time spans of their careers become, the more difficult it is for us to adequately compare one's achievement to the other. Therefore, we are seizing a special opportunity afforded to us only now at the end of the 2025 NBA season. LeBron has closed the year at age forty, and despite the delta between the number of games and seasons they each played, this is the same age at which Michael Jordan stepped off the court for the final time. No end can likely be put to the winding arguments of how these two should be compared, but this natural checkpoint provides an opportunity for a fair assessment at least on the grounds of age.

Introduction

Conversation in sports has always been laden with and perhaps even fundamentally inspired by an obsession with rankings. Sports are, after all, played to be won, and winning is the first and simplest form of ranking; each game has a winner and loser; each race has a first place, second place, third, fourth, etc. Winning status is the soul of competition, and its glory is attained instantly when the final second comes off the clock, when the final point is recorded, or when the judges declare their verdict. The quickly attained glory is, however, fleeting as another contest is always right around the corner. As the calendar marches on, each sport crowns a new champion; sometimes it is the same as the previous, yet rarely for very long. And so, after decades pass, we are always left with one ultimate metric: who was the best that year, that month, that day? This leaves us with a rankling question; is it only possible to compare players who compete head to head and moment to moment? Though it becomes difficult in many cases, the intuitive answer is, *No*. Few would contest the idea that Allen Iverson was a better player than one of the many names throughout, say, the 1960's whose coach rarely afforded him the opportunity to get up off the bench and onto the hardwood. This conviction by us all is despite the fact that the two never played against each other, nor could they ever have. We come to our conclusion through a myriad, and after a while, unconscious, set of rules and judgments, objective and subjective, that create in our minds an understanding of one's prowess in the game. This equation in full is nothing at all like the mathematics that do indeed make up a sizeable portion of its parts. In addition to the concrete and measurable, this judgment is made up also by the abacus of pneumatic, but not unimportant, things like instinct, athleticism, mystique, and legend.

This book will be characterized by two separate but indelibly connected streams of thought: that of the measurable and that of the immeasurable. The more one looks into any aspect of the game, the more apparent it becomes that nothing, even the raw, numerical accumulation of statistics, is one-dimensional, and therefore must be examined by a multifaceted mind. The sport of basketball is a fluid one, and just as its players are tasked with performing each of its moving parts throughout the game, so must we be tasked with judging each of its aspects in balance with the rest. A player's athleticism may make little impact on the game if he lacks the ball handling skills to get himself into advantageous positions. Just so, our judgment on the statistical numbers and accolades of a player means little if we lack the ability to understand why they are there in the first place.

OFFENSIVE STATS

1.
Stat Accumulation

The easiest, most basic way to understand a player's impact on the game is their scoring. This is for good and obvious reason; the team at the end of the game with the most points is the team that wins and any player's points are direct contributions to the end goal. Little time needs to be spent explaining the importance of actually putting the ball into the basket, but it must be noted and understood that scoring is often given the highest weight when people judge the importance of statistics. This priority may be assumed because while assists also indicate that your team scored, they imply a less direct contribution to the basket. After all, many more passes are completed successfully in a basketball game than shots. If any one of those passes went to a sharp shooter who, regardless of his defender's position, decided to shoot and came away successful, the assist would show up for the man who may or may not have had any intention of a basket being scored off his pass. Furthermore, rebounds and steals might be weighted even less importantly because they provide no concrete advantage on the scoreboard but rather they wipe away the opposition's opportunity to score and lay possession in the hands of one's own team. Blocks, even further down the list, may in some minds be weighed as even less important because all they really stop is a single shot on goal and rather than providing one's team with possession only create a loose ball. All of this description may seem superfluous, but its point is to give a modicum of explanation to the popular attitude that Jordan is basketball's GOAT despite the giant lead LeBron has in most statistical categories. His Airness, after all, has the reputation as one of the game's greatest scorers while LeBron James is seen as a pass-first player. These reputational assumptions are intensely influential to the opinions of large swathes of people and therefore need to be parsed and understood more on the basis of data than the rocky grounds of cultural sentiment.

Needless to say, scoring is the most intuitive single aspect of a player's performance that will show up in the box score. So, we shall start right there by asking: who scored more, Michael Jordan or LeBron James?

Well, despite scoring's crown as the most intuitive of basketball's statistics, it depends on what you mean. Cumulative scoring goes to LeBron while the points per game average goes to Jordan. But these two categories are, like everything else, more complex than such statements presume. Let's begin by examining the simple, additive category of cumulative points.

Throughout his fifteen NBA seasons, Michael Jordan racked up a total of 32,292 points. This puts him at fifth all time behind LeBron James, Kareem Abdul-Jabbar, Karl Malone, and Kobe Bryant. At the time of this writing, he stands roughly 10,000 points out of first place. At his career scoring average (which will be examined in the following section) and assuming he played 82 games per season, Jordan would have had to play an additional three and a half seasons to near that mark. Of course, in Jordan's later years when he would have been accumulating these points, he was not scoring the same as his career average of 30.1. In Jordan's final season, he averaged instead 20.0. If we generously assume that he would not have declined any further than what he was during that final season, it would have taken closer to five and a half more years to reach the current title of all time highest scorer. That title is, however, a moving target as the man in first place, LeBron James, is still playing and doing so at a high level relative to most of his peers. Due to this fact, it is fruitless to attempt a perfectly solid answer as to how far ahead LeBron is in this category; the floor of a 10,000 point gap is assured, the ceiling is unknown and its scope can only be truly judged after LeBron decides to unlace his shoes for good.

This gap is perhaps astounding to many who know Michael Jordan particularly for his proficient scoring. For the younger generations who did not get to watch the man play in real time, much or all of what they've seen is highlights which are heavily skewed towards that aspect of the game. For example, in 2024 the NBA compiled a video reel of Jordan's top sixty plays commemorating his sixtieth birthday. Of those top sixty, fifty-three were centered around scoring while the other seven were distributed among nifty passes, remembrances of an entire game's performance, and impressive or timely defensive plays. So what does it mean then that this legendary dunker and shooter of the ball is so far behind in the cumulative category? What causes it?

The obvious source for this discrepancy is in how long the two men played for. Jordan retired at the age of forty after playing fifteen seasons in the NBA. LeBron is currently in his twenty-second season but is, strikingly, that very same age of forty years old. But how? How could LeBron James be a whopping seven seasons of NBA basketball ahead of Michael Jordan? The story begins, of course, with their beginnings.

Michael Jordan was drafted by the Chicago Bulls in 1984. This was following a three year collegiate career with the North Carolina Tar Heels. We see here that nearly half of the gap between Jordan and LeBron's career length occurs as a consequence of their differences in college years. LeBron James skipped that intermediate step and went straight to the NBA after his graduation from St. Vincent-St. Mary High School in 2003. It seems odd that Michael Jordan, always billed as the ultimate competitor, did not chase after the highest level of competition that the NBA offered for a full three seasons. Perhaps it simply was not customary for players to jump straight to the biggest league on Earth as soon as they became legal adults. Indeed, it was not customary, but it had been done before, including by well known names such as Moses Malone. Maybe it is the case that Michael was simply not ready for the pros straight out of high school. That could well be understood, as even many of the all time greats did not make that giant leap. But what about after his first college year? It is the case that in both Jordan's second and third season in North Carolina he was awarded the National Player of the Year award. If the best player in the country could not move up into the NBA at the end of the 1983 season, who could? The question of why Michael Jordan decided to stay swimming in that smaller pond is a puzzling one to square with his apparent ferocity as a competitor, but it is, after all, what occurred.

These years in college put Michael Jordan at the age of twenty-one when he first stepped onto an NBA court while LeBron began the profession at just eighteen. Where then, do we get all of the other missing years from? Mixed in between Michael Jordan's first and final season in the NBA, there were four years that he did not play. These are the seasons of 1993-94, 1998-99, 1999-2000, and 2000-01. That first missed season of 1993-94 famously comes after the Chicago Bulls third consecutive championship wherein Jordan decided he had nothing else to accomplish in the sport of basketball and moved on to attempt a career in baseball. This was short-lived as he returned to the court in the following year. But this ghosted season lives on as a source of contention between those who point out its lack of seized accomplishments and those who are inclined to elevate the status of Jordan's accolades through what he *would* or *might* have achieved during its time. This same assertion of stat accumulation and/or high achievements such as MVPs or championships is less often made for the later years of hiatus (from 1998-2001), but will still come into arguments from time to time in order to shape a picture of what Jordan could have been as opposed to what he actually achieved.

Since this current line of thinking involves some speculation about what might have conceivably occurred, it may be an interesting counterpoint to argue that if LeBron decides to end his career around the same age as Jordan and is still playing quite well that we are allowed to imagine how much more he would have achieved if he continued to play another two, three, or four years, a contemplation worth considering due to LeBron's two decade demonstration of incredible durability. It's an interesting thought and perhaps worth deploying in the face of one of Jordan's dreaming fans, but for now, we will leave the speculative talk behind us.

Let us shift the focus of this point accrual to LeBron James. On February 7th 2023, LeBron did what many in the sports world had said for years was an impossibility and broke the longstanding scoring record of 38,387 held by Kareem Abdul-Jabbar. His mark has since gone on into the forty-thousands without significant signs of stopping soon. This record may in its own right see decades of time as an insurmountable achievement. To put this number in perspective, it may help to compare it to some of the other NBA greats. As of now, LeBron stands a good 4,000 ahead of the former champion Kareem, ≈ 5,250 beyond Karl Malone, ≈ 8,500 in front of Kobe Bryant, ≈ 10,000 above Michael Jordan, ≈ 10,500 higher than Dirk Nowitzki, ≈ 10,500 more than Wilt Chamberlain, and almost 12,000 clear of Kevin Durant (the only other current player to pass even the 30,000 point mark).

Lebron	Kareem	Malone	Kobe	Jordan	Dirk	Wilt	Durant
42,184	38,387	36,928	33,643	32,292	31,560	31,419	30,571

As mentioned before, part of this gulf in points between LeBron and nearly everyone else stems from his early insertion into the NBA. He played his first games at only eighteen years old, and despite the age difference he had with most of his colleagues as well as the most media pressure a young star had ever faced, the teenager from Akron, Ohio began delivering right away. By his second season in the league, LeBron was already being voted into the All-Star game, making him (at 20 years and 52 days old) the second youngest player to ever receive that honor just behind Kobe Bryant (19 years and 169 days old). Jordan was also quite phenomenal in his second season though it must be remembered that he was three years older than LeBron at that point due to his stay with the Tar Heels. This imbalance between the ages and numbered seasons that mark LeBron and Jordan's respective careers can often times create a false sense of comparison which we must work to avoid. To help illustrate this imbalance, below is a graphic showing how many NBA points each player scored from ages eighteen to forty (seasons being denoted by the age they ended that season since both players' birthdays occur during the winter months while basketball is in full swing).

Age	LeBron James	Michael Jordan
19	1,654	0
20	2,175	0
21	2,478	0
22	2,132	2,313
23	2,250	408
24	2,304	3,041
25	2,258	2,868
26	2,111	2,633
27	1,683	2,753
28	2,036	2,580
29	2,089	2,404
30	1,743	2,541
31	1,920	0
32	1,954	457
33	2,251	2,491
34	1,505	2,431
35	1,698	2,357
36	1,126	0
37	1,695	0
38	1,590	0
39	1,822	1,375
40	1,710	1,640

Immediately striking the viewer is that Michael Jordan was quite a prolific scorer when he was on the court, but counting heavily against him is the fact of multiple incomplete years including seven NBA seasons that were entirely missed out on.

When it comes to the accumulation of points there are two key ingredients; playing a lot of games and recording a lot of baskets in those games. We can glean from the graphic above that Michael Jordan often played most or all of the games in his regular seasons, a fact which is often used by some to increase the value of his shorter time window compared to LeBron. But when juxtaposed with the fact of so many incomplete and missed seasons, the amount of load put onto his body in those years of full participation becomes dampened. That is to say it is easier to play all eighty-two games when there has been a recent or is an upcoming hiatus in which to recover physically.

The largest take away the graphic above is likely to provide is in highlighting a trend of sustained excellence on the part of LeBron James and a landscape of more peaks and valleys when it comes to the career of Michael Jordan. The season of 1985-86 which Jordan started at twenty-two years old was cut short due to a broken foot that took him out for sixty-four games. The season of 1993-94 as well as a majority of the 1994-95 season was missed out on due to Jordan's stint in Minor League Baseball. These incidents are significant but relatively short compared to the time missed at both the beginning and the end of his career. The fact this elucidates is that while both players were elite scorers, LeBron was elite for a longer stretch of time and with fewer breaks in between. Such sustained excellence is necessary to harp on because the fact that he was good enough to start so early and end so late are special marks of merit in themselves. Jordan, of course, scored more total points in the seasons where both of them played a comparable amount of basketball, but that idea will be dealt with in the following section which delves into scoring on a per game basis, that is, through averages and efficiency.

2.
Per Game Scoring

An investigation into how well a player scores on a game-by-game basis must include two simple things. First, how often did they score, i.e. what is their scoring average? Secondly, how often did they succeed in scoring a basket when that was, in fact, what they attempted to do? This second facet can generally be represented through shooting averages though there are several wrinkles within the game that complicate the purity of the stat such as precise distances the shots were taken from as well as the defensive effort in guarding those shots.

Those who maintain that Michael Jordan is the GOAT will often point to his mark of 30.1 points per game over the stretch of his career. This is, in fact, the all time record in that particular statistic and a full three points above LeBron's career mark at 27.0. The fact of points per game is relatively straightforward math, and Jordan's record is indisputable. But when one looks into the details of scoring rather than the blind result there may be another story revealing itself.

Let us first look into some statistics that give an overview of each player's efficiency. An advanced metric called *true shooting percentage* is used to assess a player's actual efficiency at making their shots. Within the true shooting percentage equation is built in an adjustment for different lengths of shots since, on their face, longer shots are more difficult than shorter ones. As a general indication of their respective shooting success, it may be simple enough to display their career numbers in this stat: Michael Jordan – 56.9 TS%, LeBron James – 59.0 TS%. It should be noted that true shooting percentage does take into account a player's free throws (a stat which Jordan bests LeBron), but there is another popular advanced metric calculating only a player's shots during the flow of the game called *effective field goal percentage*. When comparing the two on this live-ball type of shooting LeBron's lead in efficiency grows even more with him at 54.8% and Jordan at 50.9%. These facts may be enough to settle a debate on who was a better shooter, but for those who are wary of the complexity of such advanced stats, we can examine things in smaller bits.

First, we must give credit where credit is due; Michael Jordan was a better free throw shooter. The career numbers put Jordan at 83.5% and LeBron at 73.7% from the penalty stripe. Jordan was also historically a better midrange shooter (roughly the same distance as the free throw line). For their careers, Jordan was a 43% midrange shooter while LeBron had a success rate of about 38% from that distance. So, the question arises: was Jordan a better shooter from any part of the floor besides that general fifteen foot mark?

It is difficult to acquire precise numbers for field goals closer to the rim since all of those shots are worth the same two points and stat keeping in the past was less thorough and robust than it is today when so many more eyes are on the court. But when it comes to available information on shots close to the basket it is little surprise that the bigger, stronger athlete is miles ahead of his competition. For data compiled on shots near the basket (five feet away or less) the King is roughly 13% more accurate than his rival. Jordan's scoring percentage on these types of shots comes in at 57.2% while LeBron James is all the way up at 70.6% for his career. If objection happens to be made about these numbers based on the fact that this takes LeBron's entire career into account while only able to study Jordan's age 33-39 seasons, then we can level the field by doing the math for that same section of LeBron's career. This would be a mistake for any detractor to make, however, as once LeBron's age 33-39 seasons are isolated, his scoring accuracy in this department does not suffer; in fact, it stays perfectly consistent.

If the paint is intuitively the territory of the larger, stronger LeBron, one might naturally assume things would look the opposite way the further away we get from the basket.

Long distance shots can be compared more evenly as the stats for three point shots have always been easy to record. Michael Jordan ended his career with a three point shot percentage of 32.7. LeBron James has so far recorded a career percentage of 35.0 from beyond the arc. While Jordan had a couple seasons of strong efficiency (one of them being 1994-95 where he played only 17 games), for nine of his fifteen seasons he shot less than 30%. In contrast, LeBron has only failed to break the 30% mark once (his rookie season which ended with 29.0). And on an interesting note about rookie seasons, there is a LeBron James who has a three point parallel with Michael Jordan though it is not the one who is the subject of our book, rather, it's his son. Bronny James just finished his first NBA season in 2025 with knocking down 9 total three pointers. This is the exact same number as Michael hit in his rookie year. The only difference is it took Bronny just 32 attempts (28.1%) while Jordan had to take 52 (17.3%).

So it seems that Jordan has the edge when it comes to the midrange but LeBron comes out on top when shooting both near and far. How is it then that Michael Jordan comes away with a higher points per game average? Is the midrange shot simply the most popular for both of them, and since Jordan is more accurate with that shot he ends up scoring more points? Not quite. The answer has a little less to do with shot selection and a little more to do with something we have only tangentially covered so far; how often each player engages in the act of shooting.

Both men being superstars in their own right, it is natural that they will be taking a majority of their team's shots compared to most other players in the league. But just how often is that? Michael Jordan for his career averaged a total of 22.9 shots per game. LeBron James on the other hand took only 19.6. This difference of 3.3 shots per game is quite a big one. Were LeBron to have taken that many more shots per contest, and assuming his career points per shot (1.38) stayed consistent, it would have raised his scoring average from 27.0 per game to 31.5, a mark that bests Jordan for the number one spot all time.

Some may be uncomfortable with conjecture of any kind even if it requires nothing but consistency in LeBron's shooting percentages. For those disconcerted people, there is another, more concrete illustration available to us which shows the truth of each man's scoring efficiency: throughout the course of his professional career, Michael Jordan took 24,537 shots for a total of 32,292 points. At the time that LeBron James took that equal number of 24,537 shots, he had already scored a total of 33,920 points (a gulf of 1,628). This gap in scoring after having taken the same number of shots is equivalent to an entire season's worth of scoring for an All-Star caliber player scoring around twenty points per game.

The answer to the above questions of why Jordan is often regarded as the superior scorer is simple; Michael Jordan scored more points per game because he took more shots per game. But outside of this fact, LeBron James has been the better all around scorer whether you're considering cumulative points, inside scoring, outside scoring, or efficiency in its broader sense; LeBron was better at everything in this department except, of course, the hallowed midrange shot.

3.
Passing

No one disputes that LeBron James was the better passer. There are few areas of the GOAT debate as cut and dry as this one. From his early days at St. Vincent-St. Mary High School LeBron James was touted as a pass-first player who was eager to get his entire team involved in the offense. A special instinct for the game made for court vision that allowed his passing skills to be as dazzling as his high flying dunks. Early comparisons to greats like Magic Johnson had some people doubtful about the authenticity of the youngster's hype, but time marched on and showed a consistent story even into the NBA where he became as much a facilitator as he was a scorer right from the jump.

A high number of assists is typically something seen for the point guard position which brings us naturally into another element of LeBron's greatness on the court. At six feet and nine inches tall and a weight around two-hundred and fifty-five pounds throughout his career, LeBron James is among the most versatile players basketball has ever seen. His tremendous size allows him to play in the post while his elite basketball IQ and handles allow him to bring the ball up the court as well. In fact, to date, LeBron James is the only player in NBA history to have been listed at some point at each of the five different designated positions. His ability to morph from wing into guard during the flow of the game and then from guard to post position continually keeps the defense scrambling on how to defend him. If the defense then decides to double team him, LeBron can use his point guard mind to find the open teammate and punish the defense with clever passes.

For his career, LeBron James averaged 7.4 assists per game compared to Michael Jordan's 5.3. Those two extra assists would have directly contributed somewhere between four and six points per game to his team's total. Aside from the edge in efficiency of LeBron's scoring discussed in the previous section, these additional baskets add directly to their team's point total in another way that is left out by the simple metric of points per game. If one were to combine points scored with points assisted on into a statistic of how many total points a player were directly responsible for, LeBron's number would then eclipse Jordan's on this new *points generated per game* basis. But for now, we'll leave scoring in the past and focus on how these players got their teammates involved.

LeBron's high assist average combined with his iron man longevity has put him in fourth place all time in accumulated assists with a total of 11,584. This is behind only John Stockton, Chris Paul, and Jason Kidd. With his current average, we could reasonably expect James to climb even further into third place if he does indeed decide to continue his career for another year or two. Michael Jordan, on the other hand, finished his career with 5,633 assists, less than half that of LeBron. This total of roughly five and a half thousand lands Jordan outside of the top fifty all time leaders for assists.

The final numbers are simply jarring. When it came to scoring we saw that Michael Jordan had a lead over LeBron in points per game, but that when the numbers were delved into, it was LeBron who ended up with the slight edge due to his efficient shooting. Here, there is no slight edge in either direction. Instead, we are dealing with a substantial difference in both per game averages and career accumulations. It is difficult to weigh the giant gap here compared to the smaller gaps in other areas, but were one to give LeBron some extra points on our imaginary scoreboard for his utter dominace of this category, it would not be entirely unfair.

4.
Rebounding

The third major statistical category to look into is that of rebounding. Few basketball fans will need a description of its importance, so we shall skip that introductory information here except to say the obvious, that rebounds grant one's team possession of the ball, simultaneously taking any scoring opportunities from the opposition. The previous section mentioned how LeBron's unique versatility aided his ability to make the correct and, often times, spectacular pass. On the flip side, his stature has also been an obvious boon when it comes to the skill of rebounding. Taller players are typically the best rebounders due certainly to their height but also to their proximity to the rim. The latter tendency of closeness to the rim, however, is not a particularly large distinguishing factor between Michael Jordan and LeBron James since both of them generally played wing positions.

Rebounding is also a statistic that heavily favors the Kid from Akron. LeBron for his career averaged 7.5 total rebounds a game whereas Michael Jordan averaged just 6.2. The accumulation over the course of their respective careers puts LeBron James at a figure of 11,731 (landing him at 26th all time in the category) while Michael Jordan collected 6,672 (this time more than half of what LeBron has accomplished, but not by a whole lot). For further evidence of rebounding consistency, we can point to the fact that Michael Jordan has only one season ever averaging at least 7.0 boards while LeBron has eighteen such years.

As we previously found in the category of passing, there is little to examine with such cut and dry statistics. Once again, there is a sizable lead on the part of LeBron James in both per game output and the total career numbers.

With the overview of the three major offensive stats behind us, there are a couple points of interest that can and should be noted. The first is that the combination of each stat (points, assists, rebounds) is a useful measure of how versatile a player's impact on the court was during a game. As a general illustration of this type of versatility, we shall introduce the number of times each man posted a triple-double in the box score. Michael Jordan's fifteen seasons ended with a total of 28 triple-doubles during the regular season and another 2 throughout his playoff runs. LeBron James, on the other hand, put up 28 triple-doubles in the playoffs alone and another 122 during regular season action. In total, this feat of all around dominance is one LeBron has accomplished five times more often than Jordan (150 to 30).

We shall not harp any longer on the offensive statistics, but the last point to be addressed is the continual question of whether the contrasting of one era against another is a fair, apples-to-apples comparison. We will see in the next chapter how changing styles of play throughout the years have changed the NBA landscape with respect to blocks per game, and the idea that small changes in the game might ripple out to create complexities for comparison is crucial to keep in mind. Therefore, we shall take a small detour to evaluate an aspect of basketball that could give one player an unfair number of bites at the apple: pace of play.

In the NBA, *pace* refers to how many possessions each team receives during an average game. There is, of course, no set number like in other sports. Rather, in basketball, the pace is determined by the current culture of the coaches and players; how fast will they take the ball up the court; how often will they let the shot clock drain down toward zero? These things have small variance from possession to possession, but when added up in the aggregate can have a large effect on what the game looks like overall. Famously, the 1970's had a pace significantly higher than other eras of basketball, and therefore offered the opportunity for higher stat lines across the league; any player who has ten to fifteen extra possessions has that many more chances to add to his stat totals.

Year	Pace	Year	Pace
1985	102.1	2004	90.1
1986	102.1	2005	90.9
1987	100.8	2006	90.5
1988	99.6	2007	91.9
1989	100.6	2008	92.4
1990	98.3	2009	91.7
1991	97.8	2010	92.7
1992	96.6	2011	92.1
1993	96.8	2012	91.3
1995	92.9	2013	92.0
1996	91.8	2014	93.9
1997	90.1	2015	93.9
1998	90.3	2016	95.8
2002	90.7	2017	96.4
2003	91.0	2018	97.3
		2019	100.0
		2020	100.3
		2021	99.2
		2022	98.2
		2023	99.2
		2024	98.5
		2025	99.1
	Ave. Pace		Ave. Pace
	96.9		94.9

Above is the NBA's pace of play alongside the years both Michael Jordan and LeBron James played. One can see that there is no enormous discrepancy in any of the comparative years like we might have seen if we included the 1970's game where years tended to end with a pace rate of well over 100. Most saliently, we see that LeBron's lead in cumulative and per game statistics cannot be attributed to a higher pace of play because it was, in fact, Michael Jordan who benefitted from more possessions during his games.

DEFENSE

5.
Blocks

Defense is among the most intriguing of all the categories we shall examine. It will be one filled with not only statistics but more intangible things such as toughness, grit, and, dare we say, fraudulency. We ought to start with the concrete to give ourselves a solid foundation for the later, more shadowy conversation.

First, let us look at the basic frames and abilities of the two stars. Michael Jordan, being 6'6" and weighing about 216 pounds, almost exclusively covered other guards. He had great defensive hands and impressive on-ball skills. But we must recognize that we are dealing with a different category of defender when we talk about LeBron James. With his 6'9" frame and heavier build of roughly 250 pounds, LeBron was known throughout the league as being a Swiss army knife whose defensive assignment was fluid and would depend on the game or possession. Despite his bulk, LeBron's legs were always remarkably agile, a combination that allowed him to defend all types of guards, wings, and centers alike. This versatility cannot be dismissed as it required the King to master several different defensive strategies at once, a feat obviously more difficult than continually facing the same type of player game after game. With that silhouetted understanding of the type of defenders they were, let us dive into the numbers a bit.

When it comes to statistics we have two basic, additive stats comparable to points, assists, and rebounds. The first of these we shall inspect is that of blocks. A player with a strong propensity for blocking the opposition's shots gives his team a twofold advantage. First, the block itself denies the offense their shot on the basket and potentially returns possession to the defense. Secondly, a player with a reputation for blocking shots can strongly influence the game by his mere presence. Opposing players who know their shot may get blocked if they approach the talented defender's territory may settle for further, more difficult shots rather than attack the basket. With that in mind, we can have a quick look at the blocking stats for each man.

Michael Jordan finished his career with a total of 893 blocks, averaging 0.8 per game. LeBron James, on the other hand, ends his age 39-40 season with 1,150 for a lifetime average of 0.7. Now, a casual fan may see those averages and immediately conclude that Jordan was a better shot blocker than LeBron James. This would mystify many due to the fact that LeBron is several inches taller and more strongly built, characteristics that typify a player with a propensity for shot blocking. There is, however, a difference in the eras the two played in that accounts for this odd discrepancy.

As anyone watching basketball throughout the ages knows, as time moves forward and the popularity of the sport widens, the potential pool from which its players are drawn gets bigger. Those young players spend more time learning the game than their predecessors, and as a result, the skill level of the average player has risen dramatically. Nowhere is this more apparent than in the area of shooting. Nowadays, nearly every player on the court is expected to be able to shoot from long distance and can even become an offensive liability if they lack the ability to stretch the floor. Because of this trend, the median distance a shot is taken from has increased. In turn, the spacing between players has also considerably increased. This subsequently leads to us having seen a general decline in blocked shots over the years. While there are outlying singular seasons, if we compare the entire careers of the both

Jordan and James, we will see this change reflected.

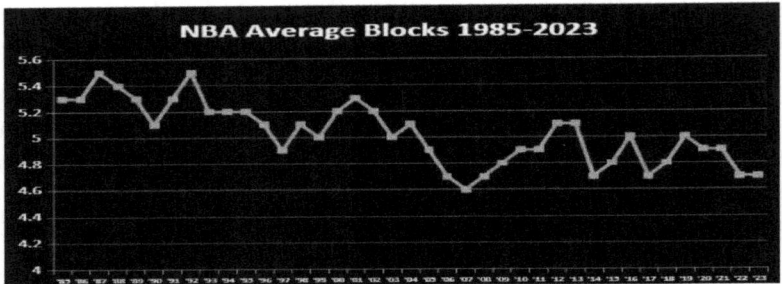

NBA Average Blocks 1985-2023

During the years that Michael Jordan played in the NBA, the league's average for blocks by a team during any given game was 5.22. The shorter shots being taken meant that the paint was condensed with help defenders who had ample opportunities to get their hands on the ball. In addition to more surrounding defenders, a short shot will tend to have a substantially lower and flatter arcing path to the basket, therefore spending more time in the air at a reachable height. In comparison, during the years that LeBron played in the NBA, the league's average blocks per game was only 4.86. Nearly half a block per game simply disappeared league-wide due to the style of play.

In addition to the evolution of skill throughout the years, there is another thing which had a substantial effect on the defense both LeBron and Jordan were able to play. This second development is that of changing rules, a topic that will be dealt with in more detail in later sections.

Hand checking's newfound illegality along with re-fined flagrant foul descriptions including things like invad-ing a shooter's landing space have made the game some-what less physical than it was in earlier decades. Usually, the loss of physicality is an injunction made by the older generation to cast aspersions on new, even quite effec-tive, styles of play. Some will argue that these rule changes make the game biased toward the offense and that the rise in scoring over the recent years is due to the rules rather than to the upgrade in skill. If someone is making this argument, they must be reminded that claiming rules have changed to make the offensive side of the ball easier nowadays is the same as saying that it is more difficult to play defense in today's game. Therefore, when comparing players from these two eras it is imperative that they each be graded in context. We simply implore the reader to be on the lookout for moments when someone attempts to diminish one era without equally diminishing its counterpoint.

When these era changes are factored in Michael Jordan's 0.1 block per game lead over LeBron gets erased, as if the concept itself was tracked down by the King and spiked into the bleachers.

6.
Steals

Through his age forty season, LeBron James has averaged 1.5 steals per game which gives him a total of 2,345. Michael Jordan averaged an incredible 2.3 steals per game, putting him at 2,514 for his career. This puts Jordan at 4th all time in steals per game behind only Alvin Robertson, Michael Ray Richardson, and Fatty Taylor. This seems like an astounding accomplishment. Anyone seeing those numbers beside each other would quite quickly determine Jordan to have been the better defender. After all, his numbers are just simply incredible. We might want to repeat that adjective one more time, *in-credible*. Yes, sadly, many in the basketball world were appalled during the summer of 2024 when Tom Haberstroh published an article scrutinizing the NBA's statistics for the season of 1987-88. What first alerted the reporter was a surprising incongruity between Michael Jordan's recorded steals and blocks depending on whether the Chicago Bulls had played at home or on the road. Closer investigation by means of reviewing available tape from some of those home games revealed a consistent inflation in Jordan's defensive stats. At the end of the season, the disparity was drastic. Both Jordan's home steals as well as his home blocks were virtually double that of those recorded on the road. This trend comes directly after Jordan had publicly criticized the voters for the Defensive Player of the Year award for basing their votes more on feel and reputation than hard box score stats. The following season then came and lo' and behold, it was eye popping numbers in the box score that won Jordan his DPOY award. The disparity over that season looked as follows: Jordan's steals at home – 165 vs. on the road – 94. Jordan's blocks at home – 84 vs. on the road 47. This turns out to be the largest difference in home and road splits ever recorded for any DPOY winner in history.

Indeed, when one zooms in on specific games this type of discrepancy reaches heights that would be comic if not for its lasting impact on our sport. During an episode of First Things First, host Nick Wright passionately explained, "There was a game against the Hawks where Michael Jordan was credited with four steals. The Hawks were credited with three turnovers. There was a game that the NBA.com has on their YouTube page right now that says 'Michael Jordan's Ten Steal Game' where the other team had nine turnovers, and the video of his ten steal game shows six steals. So I'm not saying that everything Michael Jordan won was based on a lie, but this one was."

Lest the numbers fail to convince someone of this deliberately false attribution of statistics, one can take it from Scottie Pippen himself who describes in his book "Unguarded" an incident in which one of the stat keepers vocalized their allegiance to Jordan's inflated numbers. "Here's how it worked: Say I deflected the ball and tapped it over to [Michael Jordan]. I should get credit with the steal, right? Nope. More often than not, the steal went into his column on the stat sheet, and I could do nothing about it." Pippen continues later, "One night, a scorekeeper came into the locker room after the game to hand the stat sheets to Phil Jackson and the coaching staff...I couldn't believe the look the guy gave Michael: 'See MJ, we take care of you.' No wonder in the nine full seasons we played together, he averaged more steals than me in every year except two."

Now, several people will try to make the argument that because the Bulls were not the only organization of that time recently discovered to have been padding the stats of their stars in an effort to drive narratives and entertainment that the case for Jordan's DPOY was still fair. The logic goes something like this: If everyone is cheating a bit, then we're all still on the same playing field. There are two major problems with that line of thinking. The first problem is that while it might be the case that more than one home crew was fixing stats in strange ways to increase the image of their stars, we don't have a precise handle on *how much* those figures were tampered with. Once we enter a murky topic such as an incorrectly recorded past, we run into many problems with correcting it. This matter of inflated blocks and steals (potentially assists and even rebounds as well) is not a single historical event that we can attempt to prove or disprove but rather a series of hundreds or thousands of plays where a statistic was missed or wrongly attributed. Not all of the games throughout NBA history are available for review, and even if they were, it would take a tremendous amount of man power to go back and correct the record. If the Bulls inflated Jordan's stats to a higher degree than other teams inflated their star's stats, then it still shines a proportionally negative light on Jordan despite the fact that multiple organizations were breaking the rules of integrity. The second problem with a dismissal on the basis that other teams at the time were doing the same thing is that our current conversation is not a comparison between Jordan and his contemporaries but rather one between a man in an era where teams could artificially increase their star's numbers and another man in an era where millions of people have the ability to watch and review the games and live audits and corrections to the box score are made in order to keep things fair and correct. Anyone suggesting that players simply play better at home and therefore the difference in recorded stats could be genuine need only look to the contrast between home and away stats nowadays compared to what they were in the 1980's and 1990's. For example, at the end of the 2023 season, the league-wide surplus of blocks that occurred at home was 61. Compare that to the numbers during Michael Jordan's career; a league-wide surplus of 1102 blocks in 1984 and still over 1000 in 1998. It is a sad fact to reckon with that some of the data we're forced to work with in these discussions is obviously fabricated. While we can take refuge in knowing that today's league is far more transparent, we also have to find a way to realistically come to terms with the idea that some of our games past legendary performances were just that; legend.

Since the topic of Defensive Player of the Year and its questionability has just been discussed on Jordan's part, let's turn our heads to LeBron James and the 2013 season. This was the year that LeBron made his most impactful case for the title of best defender in the league. He was playing for the Miami Heat and coming off his first championship win the year before. His defensive play was spectacular, averaging 8.0 rebounds, 1.7 steals, and 0.9 blocks per game combined with impressive on-ball defense against many of the league's best scorers. Many expected him to take home the hardware to prove his place at the top of the league, but when the votes were cast and counted an intriguing paradox unfolded. LeBron James ended up taking second place with 18 first place votes and garnering a total 149 points toward the award. The winner was declared to be Marc Gasol who received 30 first place votes and a total of 212 voting points. Now, no one would deny that Marc Gasol was a tremendous defender; what he may have lacked in pure athleticism, the bulky 6'11" center made up for with a savvy knack for the game. However, the big man's defensive play that year was less a jaw-dropping feat of personal will than it was as an important cog in a defensive machine. His 2013 team, the Memphis Grizzlies, held opponents to a significant mark of 89.3 points per game. This impressive defensive teamwork led them to having three of their players land in the top echelon of Defensive Player of the Year considerations. Gasol, of course, took first place that year while teammate Tony Allen took fifth and Mike Conley took twenty-first. In a 2020 interview, Marc Gasol acknowledges this fact and even suggests that his backcourt teammate Mike Conley may have been the one that deserved the award the most. The real kicker for Gasol's placement at the top of the DPOY list is that when other voters cast their choices for who was elected to First, Second, and Third Team All Defense in 2013 the results came out quite anomalous. One would expect that Gasol, having won the honor of best defender in the league, would have been selected for the First Team (an honor which ranks the best defender at each position league wide). Instead, it is on the Second Team that we see Gasol listed. That would be enough to raise eyebrows for most onlookers trying to get the story straight, but the strangeness is elevated further when one notes that there are six players on the All NBA First Defensive Team for 2013 instead of five. Six? But there are only five positions. Indeed, a tie in voting between Tyson Chandler and Joakim Noah placed the two of them together on the First Team list. Both men play the center position, the same one as Gasol, so according to the voters for All NBA Defensive Teams, the Grizzlies big man, despite being placed on the Second Team, was only the third best defender at his own position. This discrepancy has long raised questions about the motives and potential biases of DPOY voters especially when such legacy-changing narratives are at stake. With all of this taken into account, both Michael Jordan's highly questionable DPOY season and the one that was seemingly stolen from LeBron, the question of which player's defensive accolades rank higher than the other's is not as clear cut as Jordan fans will like to assume.

In light of the documentation of inflated defensive stats, one cannot help but wonder if this phenomenon was constrained to simply the blocks and steals already examined or if it bleeds into any other area of stat keeping. The fudging of numbers was able to occur for those defensive stats because there are several instances where who should be credited with, say, a steal is somewhat subjective since multiple players might tip the ball away from the offense before possession is secured. In such a case, the player who was most responsible for the change of possession is supposed to receive a tally in the box score, but a stat keeper looking to pump up the numbers of one particular player could theoretically hide that decision behind a thin veil of ambiguity. So, are there any offensive statistics that meet this criterion of subjectivity? The most obvious candidate is the assist. An assist is, of course, a pass to the player who scores a basket, but it is more than that. In its truest form, the assist is supposed to have some type of causal connection to the scoring of the basket. Therefore, if Player A passes to Player B and Player B makes his own move to the basket with several dribbles and pump fakes that erase any connection to the pass he received, then the basket being scored would not result in an assist for Player A. But often times there is an intermediate amount of shot creation from Player B after receiving the ball and the residual influence of the pass is seen as enough to award Player A an assist. This judgment is in the eye of the beholder, so it would be easy enough for undeserved assists to be jotted down if an unsupervised stat keeper was inclined to do so.

Not all of the games of Jordan's career are available for statistical review on NBA.com, but of those that are we found that Michael had an average of 4.91 assists recorded during home games and 4.63 for games on the road. This comparative increase for home games is interesting but much less drastic than was seen for the defensive categories. It may be a stimulating lead to follow if enough game film can be audited, but for now the discrepancy favoring Jordan's home games is probably too small to make any outright claims about. Yet the fact that does exist is an intriguing one.

WINNING

7.
Clutch?

A significant portion of the legend that is Michael Jordan is wrapped up in a certain mentality of grit and determination. The Chicago star is known as the ultimate gamer, a true competitor who always showed up when it mattered most. Sentiments such as this are clung to in the face of LeBron's overwhelming body of statistics and achievements and the intangible is elevated to a place of eminence. Well, luckily, as time has passed and the NBA has been studied by more eyes than ever, we have been graced with a plethora of information that does a lot of work in capturing these intangible characteristics. These numbers shall shed a very bright light on the topic after a brief discussion of our context.

With Michael Jordan's reputation for late game heroics laid out above, we turn our attention to the King. LeBron James' history with the ethereal idea of the *clutch gene* is among the most storied narratives in his career. As a playmaking star akin to the likes of Magic Johnson, LeBron has always made a habit of finding the most open shot. This tendency generally plays out no matter the game or situation, meaning that when the final seconds appear on the clock and the ball is in LeBron's hands he will drive or shoot if that is the best option. Otherwise, whether he gets double teamed or someone else on his squad finds an open spot on the floor, he willingly passes the ball to wherever his team stands the best chance of scoring. For many years, this playmaking attitude was frowned upon by commentators who see the last moments of a basketball game as particularly different from the rest; as a stage where the leader of a team must step forward and prove himself to be the strongest and most courageous warrior by one means alone: taking the final shot. To some, it is evidently more important to simply take the final shot in pursuit of proving one is not afraid of the moment than it is to actually make it and win the game. After all, a missed buzzer beater loses a man only one game, but a refused buzzer beater attempt makes a man a coward. This is the implicit logic of many of LeBron's late game critics. The refutation of its sentiment may be made easily enough through a critique of all similarly machismo fantasies. There are, of course, many ways to win, and a smart play is preferable to a prideful one.

All that being said, it would be wrong to assume that LeBron's willingness to make a last second pass to an open teammate means that he always gets the ball out of his hands before the moment of need. Quite the contrary. As we examine the numbers on these endgame situations, we may find a reality unfolding that is entirely counter narrative.

The first string we must tease out in this messy knot of clutch performance is precisely what we mean by being clutch. The word evolved organically in basketball terms and therefore has long lacked a distinct definition, rather it carries only a connotation of coming through when it matters the most. But depending on how one frames the situation, an understanding of when the stakes are at their highest could be vastly different. Through a pinpoint lens, this phrase may refer to simply the last shot of a game, one in where the balance of the contest is hanging. Perhaps it means the last few minutes of a game where there is more time for the pressure to build on the shoulders of the hero therefore requiring more poise to admirably perform. It may refer to the entirety of a game if that specific game holds particular value for a team chasing a desirable playoff seed or is being played against a rival whom the player must prove they can best. Or perhaps it means any one of these things but with a special weight on happening in the playoffs since the goal of the whole season is to advance as far as possible and any mistake made or opportunity missed during playoff ball would be wholly more disappointing than any similar misstep throughout the preceding eighty-two contests. It is difficult to choose only one of these subjective definitions, but to make an exhaustive inquiry of every arguable meaning would eclipse the length of this book. So, we shall pick two categories of largely differing situations while making sure to focus on the time when the pressure is greatest, the playoffs. This method aims to combine the direct application of pressure in the final minute (elimination moments) with the wider view and larger sample size (elimination games) in order to explore the reality of what we mean by *clutch*.

First on the examiner's table is the final part of a game. Zooming in to the last minute of playoff games, we can see a clear layout of shots taken to tie or take the lead. Now, in the interest of fairness, it ought to be noted that the NBA only started keeping statistics for such things in the late 1990's and therefore Jordan's earlier career is lost on us when it comes to such technical categorization. But we do have a sample size of several years from His Airness, and in these high pressure moments, Michael Jordan was 5 for 13, a success rate of 38.5%. Four of those shots were three point attempts, of which he made one, a success rate of 25%.

We have a significantly larger sample size of data for Jordan's rival. LeBron James, in the same situation of shots within the final minute of a playoff game to tie or take the lead, shot a total of 51 times. Of those, the King made 23, giving him a lifetime accuracy of 45.1% Not only are these last minute numbers in the biggest games of one's career substantially higher than Michael Jordan's, throughout all of history, LeBron's mark of 45.1% is bested by only one player, the sharp shooting Ray Allen. Protest could conceivably be made at the fact that we don't have the numbers available for the totality of Michael Jordan's career which could cause his stats to fall short of true representation. This is an understandable worry, but the Jordan fan making such a claim would do well to remember how the numbers shook out when the stats of these two men were controlled for age back in the section on scoring; the lead LeBron had on the Jumpman was not diminished by such equalized appraisal, rather it was ballooned even further.

One ought to be left dumbstruck by the contrast between the reputational narrative and the reality of these numbers. As it turns out, when the lights are brightest and when everything rides on a few seconds of performance, it is LeBron James who stands nearest the top of the mountain. We submit that the cause of this discrepancy is a simple, human error. Those who usually have reputations for this kind of clutch performance like Michael Jordan or Kobe Bryant may be acquiring it primarily through the presentation of their mentality rather than the results of their shot making. For further illustration of this point, we will make a quick deviation into Kobe's numbers for the same category. During the final minute of a playoff game, the shots the Black Mamba took to tie or win went in 12 times out of 44 attempts (27.3%). From three point range, Bryant shot only 3 for 17, a mark of just 17.6%. The total shots taken by Bryant are astoundingly comparable to LeBron's with a success rate significantly worse. Yet, the reputations of a clutch, killer mindset persist for men like Jordan and Kobe. In order for us to fairly assess complex topics such as all time rankings, we must abandon such fallacious heuristics as awarding the *clutch gene* to those who desire to take the last shot above all else, above even making it.

Now that the fairytale of LeBron's inability to take and make big shots has been thoroughly dispelled, we can zoom out to another definition of clutch performance. If a single last-minute shot does not qualify as definitively clutch due to a lack of time for the player to feel the pressure mounting on top of him, then the situation that should exemplify that idea the most is an elimination game in the playoffs. This scenario allows a day or two for the player to realize the gravity of the moments he will be on the court along with giving him an entire game's worth of opportunities to succeed or fail, therefore proving that whatever transpired in those games was not a simple fluke as any one shot might be.

The career of Michael Jordan included 13 total games. His record in those contests was sub .500 at 6 wins and 7 losses. LeBron James on the other hand took part in 29 elimination games throughout the 22 seasons we are looking at. His record in those games was 15-14, a win rate of 51.7%. But of course, despite how important winning is to one's legacy, it is at its core a team stat. If the team's success is not sufficient for showing a clutch performance, then the individual's stats will provide an undeniable answer.

By looking first at the points, we can determine each player's most direct impact on those games of dire importance. Over his 13 elimination contests, Michael Jordan averaged 31.3 points on 24.0 shot attempts, an average of 1.30 points per shot taken. LeBron James in his 29 elimination games averaged 33.1 points on 24.0 shot attempts, an average of 1.38 points per shot taken. We felt it important to include the number of shot attempts it took for each star to reach their respective points per game average since the shortcomings of only assessing total points in a game were described back in the chapter on scoring. As is plain to see, both Jordan and LeBron took almost exactly the same number of shots in such situations, and once again it is LeBron James whose efficiency rises to the top.

How about their second most direct impact on scoring, the assists? Over that same span of games, Michael

Jordan averaged 7.0 assists per game while LeBron James averaged 7.5. Given our previous examination of each man's passing skills it is no surprise that LeBron comes out ahead again.

Will there be a deviation from the pattern we've seen so far when we check on their rebounds? No. During those elimination games, Michael Jordan brought down 7.9 boards per game. LeBron James, on the other hand, comes in with a sizable lead at 10.3.

All of these stats are great, but one criticism is perhaps that, with the exception of shooting percentage, everything mentioned above only measures what each player did well under duress and does not indicate how often they cracked under the pressure and did something to actively harm their team. Many such missteps will be lost to history barring an ability to rewatch the games in their entirety, but one thing we have in hard fact is their number of turnovers. Going into games with his back against the wall Jordan averaged 4.2 turnovers. LeBron averaged 3.9. This edge for LeBron may not appear like a world of difference, but with the season on the line, every mistake is critical.

A smaller point that ought to be addressed is a few noteworthy plays often cited in attempt to tarnish LeBron's reputation. Detractors will make the claim that LeBron is disqualified or heavily sandbagged in the *clutch* category because the two biggest shots in his career were made by other people, namely Ray Allen and Kyrie Irving. Let us examine each situation on its own.

The Ray Allen shot in reference is the one made at the end of Game 6 in the 2013 NBA Finals where LeBron's Miami Heat dueled Duncan's San Antonio Spurs. The corner 3 Allen hit tied the game with just 5.2 seconds on the clock, ushering in a period of overtime where the Heat pulled out the comeback victory. It remains one of the more iconic clutch moments in NBA playoff history as it came in a pivotal moment for LeBron's legacy. There is no need to downplay Ray Allen's contribution; he was the hero of that moment. But there is more to that story than a single shot. It was said above how Allen's shot helped grasp a comeback victory for the Heat. What kind of comeback are we talking about? That famous fourth quarter started with the Heat down 65-75. With a ten point deficit and his back against the wall of elimination, LeBron James took over. Dwyane Wade was on the bench for most of the quarter, requiring LeBron to score or assist on 23 of the Heat's 27 points leading up to the moment in question. All of this offensive dominance occurred while simultaneously shutting down the Spurs' backcourt engines in Tony Parker and Manu Ginobili and recording a momentum swinging block at the rim against the great Tim Duncan. James then went on to score or assist on every point the Heat scored in overtime until the final seconds where San Antonio was forced to foul. So, while Ray Allen did rise to the occasion with a heroic shot in a giant spot, it was sandwiched between two sustained runs of brilliance by LeBron James which can only go overlooked if one's intent is specifically to do so.

The second big shot of note is the one made by Kyrie Irving near the end of Game 7 in the 2016 Finals. LeBron's Cavaliers were playing against the 73-9 Golden State Warriors and attempting to complete the first comeback ever down 1 game to 3 in the NBA Finals. Kyrie's famed shot came after a defensive switch forced Steph Curry into on-ball defense. Irving capitalized on that favorable matchup by hitting a three-point wing shot with 53.0 seconds left on the clock. There are a few things about this situation that should be taken into consideration when faulting LeBron for letting a teammate sink such an important bucket. The first is that it would be erroneous to pretend that this was the only noteworthy play made by the Cavaliers at the end of this game. Anyone with a modicum of NBA knowledge knows that just a few possessions removed from this shot is perhaps the single most iconic defensive play in NBA history; we're talking, of course, about LeBron James' chase down denial of Andre Iguodala's would be layup. Of all the defensive stands made in the annals of basketball, this is at the pinnacle in every sense. To dismiss this aspect of LeBron's clutch play in the game would simply be to deny reality. Again, the story is incomplete if assessing this game's clutch factor through the lens of one single play. Much like the game against the Spurs, it was LeBron James who was the overwhelming engine for the Cavaliers' offense late in that game. Leading up to the shot by Kyrie, James had scored or assisted on 12 of Cleveland's last 14 points. It was LeBron who brought the team back from their earlier deficit and allowed Kyrie's shot to mean what it meant. And it must be said that we mean to take nothing away from Kyrie Irving's performance, but in a conversation about clutchness, it's only fair to acknowledge that the shot he hit was not the final one of the game nor, since things were tied up at 89, were the Cavaliers facing the immanent end of their season should he miss. Any attempt to assert that Kyrie was the clutch one on the Cavs team that day must contend with these facts.

As much as we want to point out the truth of LeBron's clutch play in these examples, we cannot forget to give credit where credit is due. His teammates, Ray Allen and Kyrie Irving here but many more throughout his storied career, did rise up and perform their best in their biggest moments. We should laud them for it, and when one is talking about a span of twenty or so years, we should expect a certain amount of assistance to occur. Basketball is, after all, a team sport, and no one player does it all alone. Even the greatest one-on-one players, the tenacious competitors of our game, have had teammates step up and win games for them. And Michael Jordan is no exception.

We can go right back to the high stakes of the NBA playoffs in 1997 when the Bulls faced off against the Utah Jazz. It was Game 6 and the score was knotted up at 86 apiece. Chicago had the ball as time was expiring and Michael Jordan made a move to drive. However, unable to get fully past his defender and with another man coming to double, Jordan passed the ball to a cutting Steve Kerr who spotted up near the top of the key. Kerr's leaning jumper hit nothing but net and the Bulls went up by 2 with just 5 seconds left in the game. The shot was the talk of the town. Kerr induced a hearty laughter for the sports world at a subsequent celebration of their title with a ribbing tale of Jordan's fear of the moment and request for the sharp shooter's assistance. With such a shot occurring in the biggest possible scenario and the spotlight following it afterwards, one would imagine that those arguing for the supremacy of Jordan's career would remember it. But as time goes on, these somewhat ancillary facts seem to fade.

Perhaps this fact dwindled in the minds of some because it was only an isolated incident rather than a pattern. Unfortunately, that cannot be the case either. LeBron's career has two moments of heroic teammate baskets. And so does Jordan's.

The other even more forgotten shot came from the hands of John Paxson in Game 6 of the 1993 Finals. With Chicago down 2 and only 14 seconds on the clock, the Bulls marched the ball up the floor. Michael Jordan pushed the ball ahead, passing off to Scottie Pippen. After a quick series of inside-outside passes, the ball came to John Paxson who did not hesitate from the left wing, letting fly a gorgeous three-pointer. The clock ticked down to 3.9 seconds as Paxson's shot splashed through the hoop and swung the Bulls from a loss to a championship title.

It is not the contention of this book that we should hold these plays against Michael Jordan. There is no reason to expect in a game of five-on-five that all the central plays would be made by one person no matter how talented that individual may be. But for those out there who would like to hold such things against a player's reputation by claiming LeBron was saved in the Finals by his teammates twice in twenty-two seasons, it should be remembered that Michael Jordan's teammates saved him in the

Finals twice in just fifteen.

So, it seems that no matter which way the data are sliced, the same answer comes out every time. LeBron James is not only more accurate with his final shots than Michael Jordan was but he made a higher total tally of them too. And when it comes to games that a man walks into with the pressure of the world on top of him, it is LeBron James whose team came out the better more often, LeBron James who scored more points, assisted on more baskets, collected possession more often off the board, and gave the ball to the opposition more seldom. Despite the narrative in the minds of some, it is Le*Clutch* who always comes through.

8.
Overview On Team Wins

Aside from all of the individual stats, what may be the highest contributor to the public's understanding of what makes a good player is simply how often they win. That is, after all, the primary goal every player harbors when he steps out onto the court. If we were to witness a talented player passing up open teammates under the basket to instead take a contested jump shot all in the name of racking up a high amount of points for himself, we would not only think he was a poor team member but we would also hold such a style of play against him when calculating how impressive his personal scoring was. Every great competitor must play to win the game.

Then again, this category alone is also potentially misleading as the sport of basketball is highly dependent on the talent and cohesion of one's team as a whole. Five reasonably competent players can easily dispatch of an opposition consisting of one all time great and four incompetent players or even simply a team of talented pieces that does not fit together in a complimentary way. That in mind, we must examine winning on a particular scale; how often did a player win and with what kind of team make up around them (including the teams they played against).

Starting with the most basic numbers, Michael Jordan had an all time regular season win/loss record of 706-366, a winning percentage of 65.9%. LeBron James in the regular season ended with an all time record of 1,009-553, a percentage of 64.6%. In the playoffs, Michael Jordan was 119-60, a playoff win percentage of 66.5%. LeBron's playoff record is currently 184-108, a success rate of 63.0%. After thousands of regular season games and hundreds of playoff games, these are remarkably similar win rates especially when one considers Jordan's reputation as a winner above all else and the polemics against LeBron's ability to finish games and seasons (partially dispelled in the previous section).

Single games, however, are not necessarily the only metric for measuring a player's winning success. The NBA playoffs, being grouped into multiple series, provide another significant measurement. The more series a player wins, the more often they have approached the ultimate goal of winning a championship. In Michael Jordan's career, he played 37 total playoff series and won 30 of them, an 81.1% win rate. LeBron's career series record through age 40 is 41-14, a win rate of 74.5%. Now, it is imperative to be noted that several of Michael Jordan's series losses came in the first round and up until the year 2005 the NBA only played a best of 5 game series in that round instead of the current best of 7. That means that any playoff series Jordan lost in the first round (3) effectively took the same number of losses away from his career total when proportionally compared to LeBron's. This means if Michael had played in today's 7 game series format, those first round losses would most likely drag his win percentage down in turn. Furthermore, it is only fair to assume the Bulls still would have lost those series as none of them were particularly close.

If we look at the source of most Michael Jordan GOAT arguments, it is in comparing their NBA Finals records. Jordan boasts a famous 6-0 record whereas LeBron's stands at 4-6.

There are several threads to tease apart in judging what a team winning stat means for the individual. Each of these threads will be dealt with in subsequent chapters, starting with an inquiry into their playoff success followed by examinations of the teams they played for and against.

9.
Playoff Success

Without question, when the GOAT topic is brought up in media debates or casual discussions, the most common argument put forth for Jordan comes out as a pithy "6-0." It has become the most popular evidence of Jordan's supposed superiority largely due to the perceived brevity of its core message. But despite its presumed simplicity, it is really two statements wrapped up in one. The first is this: Michael Jordan won 6 championship rings. The second is this: Michael Jordan never lost in the NBA Finals. These two implicit statements come as a comparison to LeBron James and his Finals record of 4-6. The key in dealing with this line of argument is to separate the two implicit statements and recognize them for their differing levels of legitimacy.

The first embedded meaning of the "6-0" idea comes from that first number. It is the lesser of the two problems for the simple fact that winning a championship is a wonderful thing and ought to be celebrated. Just over six hundred total human beings in the history of the world can claim the title of NBA champion. This is an astonishingly great feat. There have been several billion people walking the Earth since the NBA's conception, and most of them will not sniff such an accomplishment. It is only the top of the top even in the narrow world of basketball who can ever claim a number higher than zero in that first column. The second column, the 0, on the other hand, is a different story. It is in some sense the exact opposite story. Take those billions of people just mentioned. None of them have lost in NBA Finals either. They are tied with the great Michael Jordan! The collective record for the laymen of the world in the NBA Finals is 0-0, and zero is a very strange number. Due to its often ethereal nature of non-value, it can imply things that turn out to be quite different than a phrase's actual meaning.

That second column, the Finals losses, is just that. It describes only what occurred within the confines of the NBA Finals. In a trip of reverie, one might wish to cordon off reality in such a specific way to highlight certain moments, but the basketball season, and indeed reality as a whole, cannot be so divorced from the rest of time. Having 0 losses in the NBA Finals does not mean that one did not lose at the game of basketball. It simply denotes a very specific way of saying where one *did not* lose. That is to say, an NBA player who did not lose in the Finals is left with three other options broadly speaking. They could have been the winner of the championship, they could have lost in the playoffs before the Finals began, or they could have missed the playoffs entirely. For most every NBA player, the end of the season comes with the happenstance of not having lost in the Finals. It would be a great deal more informative to abandon this method of speaking in the negative and talk about playoff success in a way that reveals precisely how far a player made it in the playoffs each year they did not win the Finals. Refusing to put things in these terms would be tantamount to a strange reversal of logic where a player who wins considerably more games en route to losing in the Finals is penalized compared to a player who won few or even no games at all but thereby keeps his tally of Finals losses at 0. So, when they weren't winning the NBA Finals what is it Michael Jordan and LeBron James were doing?

The story of years Michael Jordan did not win the NBA title starts awfully dismal. The first three seasons of his career end by being bounced in the very first round of the playoffs, two of which were sweeps, 0 games to 3. He then followed these three disappointing exits with two second round losses in 1988 and 1994, two more third round Eastern Conference Final exits in 1989 an 1990, and then two seasons where he missed the playoffs entirely in 2002 and 2003.

Turning our heads to LeBron James' tale of playoff exits, we start with three first round losses in 2021, 2024, and 2025. For second round defeats there are a total of three including 2006, 2008, and 2010. Teams led by LeBron were bounced in the Conference Finals twice during 2009 and 2023. Four seasons in total have occurred where LeBron's team missed the playoffs. The first two occur during his rookie and sophomore seasons while the other two come toward the tail end of his career in 2019 and 2022. While this total of four missed playoff berths is more than Jordan's two, it should be noted that the first two happened when LeBron was 19 and then 20 years old. When we remember that Michael Jordan spent his age 19 and 20 seasons in college we can put this into perspective by saying that while LeBron may have missed the NBA playoffs those years, Jordan missed the NBA altogether. The 2019 miss also requires a bit of context since it occurs during the period of time where LeBron James suffered the only really significant injury of his career. A torn groin in the middle of the year took LeBron out of action for 17 consecutive games. The Lakers were in 4th place in the Western Conference when the injury occurred but quickly fell down the rankings with his absence. James returned before he was fully recovered which led to a decision in March to rest him for the remainder of the season to allow his body true healing time.

The graph below indicates where LeBron and Jordan ended their seasons in years they did not win the NBA title from ages 18-39.

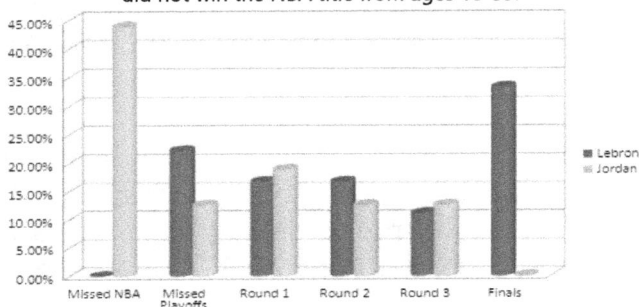

With all of their non-championship seasons beside each other, it is clear to see that LeBron James had a greater rate of success in the playoffs in general despite a higher number of rings from Jordan. Of his 22 seasons, LeBron made it to the Finals 10 times, a rate of 45.5%. Jordan's 15 seasons resulted in 6 trips to the Finals, only a 40.0% appearance rate. Their respective success on the graph shows a general trend of longer playoff runs for LeBron James and a pattern of quicker exits for Michael Jordan. These are the kinds of facts implicitly shrouded behind the obscurity of the zero in the "6-0" phrase, and until the basketball world can commit to leaving such foolish logical framing in the past, we will be stuck running around in circles as continuous as the number 0 itself.

10.
Jordan's Team Strength

As has been mentioned several times, winning, though it is the primary objective of any individual player during any game, is first and foremost a team stat. Great individual players like Wilt Chamberlain have had seasons with unbelievably gaudy individual numbers, but without a cohesive team, the main goal of the game fell out of his reach in comparison to some of his contemporary peers. There is no one objective way to measure the strength of talent any single team employs nor is there a straightforward measure of how well those players work together to create a championship caliber group. In lieu of these numerical statistics, we will have to rely on a multitude of factors such as awards, statistical averages, ages of players, coaching experience, and the overall success of each teammate throughout their careers.

This multitude of data will be more easily done for Michael Jordan as the fifteen year veteran played most of his seasons (and really all of his impactful ones) for the same team with much of the same key make up surrounding him. LeBron James, on the other hand, having played for seven additional years and for three different franchises, will require a larger patchwork of constituents to create an overall image of team strength throughout his success.

In the following analysis, we will be looking only at the team composition of years where either Michael Jordan or LeBron James succeeded in winning the NBA Championship. A comprehensive look at team strength spanning every single year of their careers would, due simply to the number of players involved, likely require a book of its own. Therefore, in the interest of examining first and foremost the teams that contributed to each player's winning, strength of team will be primarily defined in this way.

While the players on the court understandably get the lion's share of the glory in a championship win, it ought to be acknowledged that a team's construction goes several levels beyond those wearing the jerseys. There are team owners who hire much of the staff and provide resources and facilities; there are managers who oversee the operations of the team and put untold hours into drafting and trading pieces to improve their squad; and there are a plethora of coaches involved from the individual positional and skill coaches all the way up to their chief, the head coach. For the sake of time and immediate influence on the game, we shall focus on the head coach as the locus of organizational proficiency.

For each of the years that Jordan won a championship with the Bulls, Chicago employed Phil Jackson as head coach. This name will not be new to anyone who has more than a cursory familiarity with the NBA as Jackson spent two full decades coaching in the league. A simple listing of Phil Jackson's accomplishments may be enough to give an impression of the excellence he continually produced. Jackson stands with an amazing 11 championship titles, the most out of any coach in the history of the NBA. The astonishing accomplishment of 11 titles in 20 years is unparalleled in basketball. More than half of the time that Phil Jackson coached a team, that team would end up hoisting the Larry O'Brien trophy. Fans of Jordan's then, who tout his absolute dominance of winning 6 rings in 15 years, might think better by looking at the resumé of the Bulls' mental and strategic leader. His migration from Chicago to Los Angeles also proves that his success was not only due to the strength of the specific organization around him.

In addition to his championships, Jackson is 7th in all time wins as a head coach, a mark that he likely would have improved on if he'd spent more time in the league like his peers above him such as Gregg Popovich who currently resides in the top spot after a 26 year career. It is also imperative to point out that in the five years before Phil Jackson became Michael Jordan's head coach, the Bulls finished the regular season under .500 three times. In fairness, we have to subtract much of the 1985-86 season since Jordan broke his foot and only played 18 games. But even in that stretch Chicago was a less than impressive 7-11. Then in the years that Jordan played for the Washington Wizards (the only other years that Phil Jackson was not his team leader) Michael had a total record of 74-90, another sub .500 performance. All together this gives Michael a regular season record of 256-254 without the direct tutelage of Phil Jackson. That woeful record is complimented by the fact of just three total playoff series victories. Of course, these stints of time were toward the beginning and end of Jordan's career, but nevertheless, it is entirely the case that without Phil Jackson around not only did Michael Jordan not win a championship but he was hardly even a winning player.

As influential as coaching is, the people truly in the spotlight are the members of the team running, sweating, and fighting out the games. When it comes to the prowess of one's teammates nowadays it is usually LeBron James who receives criticism for playing alongside the likes of certain stars like Dwayne Wade, Chris Bosh, and Anthony Davis. While no one will deny the skill of any one of these players, the crucial aspect of this teammate relationship should not be simply the perceived talent of one's teammates but rather the measure of how much they contributed to the team's winning compared to our focus player (Jordan/James). In the history of the NBA, there have been a laundry list of superb teammates such as Shaq and Kobe, Magic and Kareem, Steph and Klay. But among the very top of those ranks must sit Jordan and Pippen, a Batman and Robin combination whose skills worked in fantastic unity and allowed both to reach maximum potential.

Michael Jordan's first championship ring was won in the 1990-91 season. His chief running mate, as always, was the renowned jack of all trades, Scottie Pippen. Pippen had joined the team straight from the draft after he was taken by the Seattle SuperSonics and quickly traded to Chicago in 1987. This turned out to be a tremendous, and immediate boon to Michael Jordan who, only after receiving Scottie Pippen as a right hand man, was now able to get out of the first round of the NBA playoffs. Indeed, until Pippen arrived in Chicago, Jordan only succeeded in winning one single playoff game in his previous three seasons.

While Michael Jordan led the team in scoring that first championship year, it was Pippen who was the duo's leader in assists, rebounds, and blocks throughout the course of the season. This trend would continue with Pippen acting in the Batman role of these categories while Jordan did most of the scoring. During several of their championship years, Pippen would also best Jordan in steals, earning this ultimate Robin perennial consideration for Defensive Player of the Year. Scottie did so much on the court, in fact, that in a television interview midway through the Bulls' dynastic run, coach of the team, Phil Jackson, uttered the words "Scottie is such an unselfish player. He's the greatest all around player in the NBA right now." When the reporter offered a sentiment on Jordan's elite scoring capabilities Jackson replied with, "Now, Michael, no one can score like Michael, and scoring's a wonderful thing to do, but it's not the end all end all..."

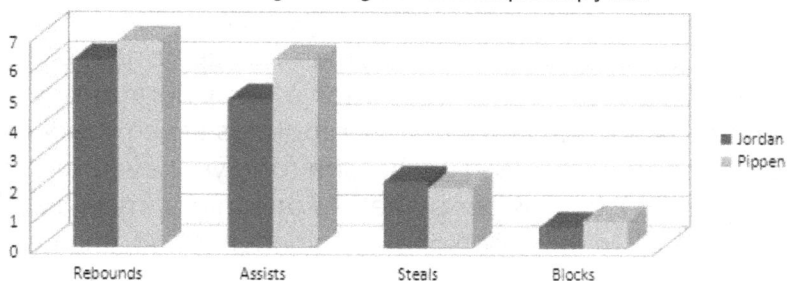

With Scottie Pippen being among the best and most well-rounded players in the game at the time, the Bulls have set Jordan up with a fantastic foundation. There is perhaps no ability more cherished in one's second in command than the skill and knowledge to do everything at a reasonably high level. That way, any time the star is performing poorly in a given area there is someone there to pick up the slack. But there is far more to the story of Chicago's domination of the 1990's than a simple Batman and Robin.

As said above, Jordan's playoff success had not left the ground at all until after Scottie Pippen arrived in Chicago, but later on there were more additions that took the Bulls from a team with a dominant duo to a team that excelled in every single area. Perhaps the piece that stands out the most (for several colorful reasons) is the acquisition of Dennis Rodman.

Rodman had previously played for the Detroit Pistons and spent a quick two years in San Antonio before the 1995-96 season rolled around and he was picked up by Chicago. While Michael and Scottie under the tutelage of Phil Jackson had been enough to win three championships in the earlier part of Jordan's career, the Bulls historic dominance set in after the acquisition of The Worm. Rodman brought a toughness and grit to the Bulls that had seldom been seen before in the game of basketball. Despite a height of only 6'7", Dennis Rodman was a tenacious rebounder. The likes of his skill on the glass is something the NBA has rarely if ever reproduced since his retirement in 2000. Simply put, Dennis Rodman was demonstrably the best rebounder in the league for a long duration of his career. He led the NBA in total rebounds seven years in a row starting in the 1991-92 season (one year averaging as many as 18.7 boards per game). As one might immediately notice, this streak of personal dominance for Rodman runs straight into the heart of Jordan's championship years. Aside from simply rebounding, Dennis Rodman was a very capable defender earning him Defensive Player of the Year votes (7th place and 5th place) in two out of the three years he played for Chicago. Since rebounding tends to take place closer to the basket and on-ball defense tends to take place further from the basket, Rodman's years of re-bounding dominance and his years of DPOY awards (1989-90, 1990-91) are necessarily separated, but his ability to do either one depending on the moment did not wane.

So far, in our inquiry into what made the 1990's Bulls so dominant and led to Jordan's six championships, we have examined the strategic edge and leadership they had in Phil Jackson's coaching, the proliferate scoring of Michael Jordan, the ultimate Swiss army knife in Scottie Pippen, and one of the great defenders and rebounders the game has ever seen in Dennis Rodman. One of the only spots on the floor not expertly covered by any of these men is the outer perimeter. But just like every other aspect of the game, the Chicago Bulls were not lacking in this department.

In 1993, the Bulls brought in Steve Kerr from Orlando. He went on to play for the Bulls from then until 1998 when he joined the San Antonio Spurs. Coming off the bench, Kerr received consideration for 6th Man of the Year in both the 1993-94 season as well as in 1995-96. But perhaps the key element in Kerr's contribution to the Bulls' machine of war was his long-distance sharp shooting. Famously, Steve Kerr ended his fifteen years of professional basketball with a final shooting percentage of 45.4% from behind the arc. To this very day it remains the highest three-point shooting percentage for any player's career since the first arcing line was painted in 1979. Granted, the number of three-point shots taken back in the 1990's was significantly fewer than in today's game, but the point remains that in the era of Jordan's championships, the Chicago Bulls had the league's most accurate marksman. Aside from the obvious points that hitting a three-ball awards, having a lethal shooter from long distance provides a strong benefit to the offense as a whole since defenders have to stick closer to, or be more aware of, the potential shooter, therefore leaving more space open for interior players to post up, cut, and penetrate on the dribble. Having the league's all time most accurate shooter on their team allowed the Bulls to take advantage of an amount of offensive space afforded to few other teams.

This preceding list of coach and players is certainly not exhaustive when it comes to the contributors to Jordan's success in those six championship years, but it does highlight the combination of talent and team construction that made up the dominant Bulls. Not only were each of these key pieces placed at different positions, allowing them to work to their specialized strengths, but they were almost undoubtedly each the best in the league at their job. It must be stressed that we are not contending each Bulls player was the best of all time at what they did but rather that they were the best or among the best in the league at the time. No one would reasonably suggest that in the grand scheme of things Steve Kerr was a better three-point shooter than Steph Curry despite the fact that his career percentage is higher. We can all recognize that the more the three-point shot got integrated into the league's style of play, the more shots were taken from that distance and defenders came further out to make those shots more difficult. But when it comes to contributing to Jordan's championships, the fact that Steve Kerr played heavy minutes as such a lethal shot maker compared to most of his contemporaries was a great boon to the Bulls. That in mind, a short recap of what Chicago was putting on the court each night during Jordan's championships reveals the best coach in the league at the time (and perhaps the best in history) in Phil Jackson, the best two-way, right-hand man in the league (and arguably of all time) in Scottie Pippen, the best rebounder in the league (and perhaps on a pound for pound basis the best of all time) and perennial DPOY candidate in Dennis Rodman, and the most accurate distance shooter in the league (and in one sense still to this day) in Steve Kerr. This is all in addition to the man who most considered the best scorer and best player in the game at the time, Michael Jordan. The fact that this fully assembled team whose top pieces complimented each other so perfectly won three championships could hardly surprise.

But perhaps we've been unfair. After all, Jordan was the center of the team, the engine, correct? Some of what is described here is fantastic role players and a historically good head coach. If Michael Jordan, their undeniable leader, was removed from the equation, could they possibly be a success? Luckily, we have a case study that illuminates just this question. During the 1992-93 season, Jordan won his third championship with Chicago after going 57-25 in the regular season. He then took a year's hiatus to play minor league baseball. However, the Chicago Bulls continued playing basketball. Without the help of their star player, the ultimate competitor and scorer, His Airness, the Bulls finished the 1993-94 season with a record of 55-27, just two fewer wins than the year before. Is that all Michael Jordan was worth? Of course, that would be ridiculous to say; the Bulls did not go on to win the championship and perhaps they would have if Jordan were there to keep the team as it had been the three previous years. Instead, Chicago won their first round match up against the Cleveland Cavaliers and ended up losing out in a tight Eastern Conference Semifinal series against the Knicks 4 games to 3. But the overarching point is that the Bulls were still a team winning nearly sixty games and competing for championships even without Michael Jordan. The same will not be seen in the next section when we take a look at the teams LeBron James acted as engine for. While Jordan got to be the most important gear in a finely tuned machine, LeBron James was the whole frame, without which little could stand.

11.
LeBron's Team Strength

In the previous section, we began our assessment of the team surrounding Michael Jordan by looking at the tactical head of that organization, Phil Jackson. Doing this for Jordan was relatively simple whether it be for all his seasons or strictly his championship ones since Jackson was Michael's coach for all of his winning years. LeBron James on the other hand, has had a litany of head coaches by virtue of the fact that he has played for three different franchises and one of them, the Cleveland Cavaliers, he played for at two different points in his career. Thankfully, only the coaches who presided over his four championships will be dealt with in any detail in this section, but as a point of interest we are compelled to mention that of the ten NBA coaches the King has played for in his career (Silas, Malone, Brown, Spoelstra, Blatt, Lue, Walton, Vogel, Ham, and Reddick), none of them have won even a single championship ring without LeBron James on their roster.

LeBron's first NBA title came as a member of the Miami Heat in 2012 with Erik Spoelstra in the role of head coach. The same is true of his second title when the Heat repeated their run in 2013. Spoelstra began his tenure as head coach in Miami in 2008 and has remained at that post to this day. Widely respected around the league, Spoelstra has done an impressive job of getting to the Finals six times. However, four of those six appearances and the only two championships he has won occurred with LeBron James as his star player.

The third time LeBron hoisted the Larry O'Brien trophy was in his remarkable return to the Cleveland Cavaliers after leaving them for Miami a few years prior. The story of who was head coach for the Cavaliers in 2016 is an odd one as the season began with David Blatt at the helm. In January of that year, however, Blatt was fired and replaced with then assistant coach Tyronn Lue. In professional sports, a midseason coaching change usually indicates such organizational strife that the idea of winning a championship any time soon, let alone that very same season, seems somewhere between farfetched and ludicrous. Tyronn Lue, having less than a year's experience as a head coach by the time the 2016 Finals came around became one of the greenest coaches in history to write their name in the book of champions. He went on to make it to the Finals twice more in the two following years with LeBron James leading the Cavaliers. Other than those three years, Lue has not won or even reached another NBA Finals as a head coach.

LeBron's fourth NBA title came on the west coast after he had elected to join the Los Angeles Lakers. The season of 2019-20 was another one fraught with unique circumstances. This time instead of a single team's coaching change, it was the entire league that dealt with adversity when play was abruptly suspended midseason in response to the Covid-19 pandemic. Once stadiums were emptied and new guidelines delineated, the NBA resumed and the playoffs were held in Orlando where the players could live in facilities separate from their families and the rest of society as they fought out the end of the season. The coach for the Lakers during this tumultuous time was Frank Vogel. Vogel had previously had stints in Boston, Philadelphia, and Indiana as an assistant coach from 2001-11. He then rose up to the head coach position for the Pacers during the 2010-11 season and remained a head coach until 2024, working for Indiana, Orlando, Los Angeles, and Phoenix. Only once did Vogel ever win or appear in an NBA Finals series; that was, of course, in Orlando's Covid-19 Bubble with LeBron James in his huddle.

So, to recap the history of LeBron James' championship coaches, there have been three men described, none of whom has won an NBA title without LeBron on their roster out of the combined 38 seasons they have spent in the league. Only twice out of those 38 did one of those coaches even reach the Finals without LeBron (Spoelstra), and in one of those two appearances was beaten by LeBron while he was a member of the Los Angeles Lakers. It can therefore be thoroughly determined that while coaching was a great advantage for Jordan's Bulls, it was never a particular strong point (and often a weak one) for LeBron's teams.

With the coaching behind us, let us shift attention to those notable names who took the court beside the King. No matter whose career we might follow, any span of twenty years in the NBA is likely to include dozens of noteworthy teammates. This is undoubtedly the case for LeBron James, but the list is laden with necessary context. For instance, one of LeBron's teammates in Cleveland was Shaquille O'Neal, an all time great at the center position. Of course, the Big Diesel at that point was closing in on end of his career and nowhere near the championship form of his earlier years in Los Angeles. Despite his enormous name, no one counts Shaq as one of LeBron's most significant teammates for this reason. The same can be said of other stars such as Derrick Rose, Dwight Howard, and Carmelo Anthony. Instead, the men who contributed most to LeBron's winning are usually proposed to be Dwyane Wade, Chris Bosh, Kyrie Irving, Kevin Love, and Anthony Davis.

Taking these men in chronological order with respect to when LeBron won championships with them puts Dwyane Wade first on the block. LeBron and The Flash won two NBA titles together in 2012 and 2013. Wade is generally considered to be LeBron's best all time teammate, and if there is any dispute when comparing the talent of those candidates then there is no dispute about their accomplishments. Wade was a perennial All-Star selection throughout the peak of his career as well as a recipient of votes for MVP and DPOY in several different seasons, though he never did win any of those awards. His biggest single accomplishment was in 2006 when he led the Miami Heat in scoring en route to an NBA championship. The duo of Wade paired with Shaquille O'Neal bested the Dallas Mavericks in a contentious 6 game series where Wade was awarded the Finals MVP trophy. While Wade was a talented scorer and even led the league in that category in the 2008-09 season, his scoring dropped a notable amount in the years LeBron joined Miami as the pair found that their styles of play were too similar to congruently fit on the court together without concerted adjustment. Wade made the humble decision to step back a bit and let LeBron (though he was the newcomer to Miami) take the reins on team leadership. After this occurred, the two went on to win championships in back to back seasons during which Wade averaged 21.7 points, 4.9 rebounds, 4.9 assists, 1.8 steals, and 1.1 blocks.

Famously, the Miami Heat's big three was rounded out by the former Raptor, Chris Bosh. Bosh, another player to continually show up in All-Star games throughout his glory years, played third wheel to the dynamic duo of LeBron and Wade. Much like the clash in style James had with his Robin, Bosh's midrange face-up game took up the same space on the floor as his co-stars therefore causing a further adjustment period for the three to figure out how to remold their games into a cohesive unit. Though an 11 time All-Star, Bosh only ever received votes for MVP in two seasons as a Raptor in which he finished 7th and 12th and was never considered for Defensive Player of the Year. During the years in question where the Miami Heat won their championships, Bosh finished the seasons averaging 17.3 points, 7.4 rebounds, 1.8 assists, 0.9 steals, and 1.1 blocks.

With the Miami years in the rearview, we move on to LeBron's second stint in Cleveland when the Kid from Akron returned to his hometown to deliver them their first ever NBA championship. Many polemicists in search of tarnishing LeBron's legacy will refer to this situation as another "super team" with a big three of LeBron James, Kyrie Irving, and Kevin Love. Again, this is a label without any clear definition, so we will have to burrow into the facts to see if such a claim has legs.

If either Kyrie Irving or Kevin Love were the Robin to LeBron's Batman in those Cleveland years, it was undoubtedly Kyrie. The ball-handling wizard was young, exciting, and had a flirtatious demeanor toward the spotlight. It was Irving's fifth year with the Cavs after they drafted him in 2011. He had been voted into 3 All-Star teams in the years before but conspicuously was not a selection in 2016. Throughout that championship season, Kyrie averaged 19.6 points, 3.0 rebounds, 4.7 assists, 1.1 steals, and 0.3 blocks per game. This stat line was enough to help LeBron toward his third, and Kyrie's first, NBA title. In fact, it stands to this day the only championship ring Irving has ever secured. His only other Finals appearance without LeBron as a teammate came in 2024 with the Dallas Mavericks as he played behind the European phenom Luka Doncic.

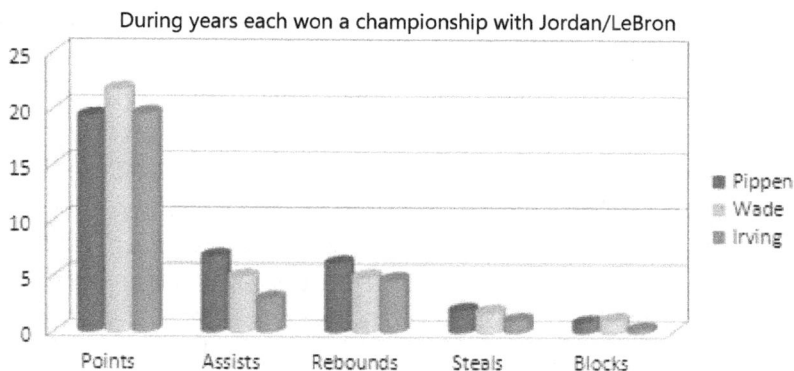

With all due respect to Kyrie Irving, this performance as a Robin seems to pale in comparison to what we saw Scottie Pippen achieved in the previous section in the same role for Michael Jordan. If that is the case, then the third member of LeBron's "big 3" must have been substantially better than Rodman if we are to believe that the Cavaliers were a super team of All-Stars but the Bulls were not. That third member is of course Kevin Love. The big man had come from Minnesota in 2014 after six years as a Timberwolf. Just like Kyrie Irving, Love had been named to three All-Star games previous to the 2015-16 season. He had also received votes in both 2012 and 2014 for MVP but finished just 6th and 11th respectively. Despite a more productive past in Minnesota, Love's championship year with the Cavaliers went by without an All-Star selection, and he finished the season averaging 16.0 points, 9.9 rebounds, 2.4 assists, 0.8 steals, and 0.5 blocks. When comparing this to Rodman's production alongside Jordan we see that Love scored around 5 more baskets per game while Rodman pulled down roughly 5.5 more rebounds. Each man also possessed non-statistical talents the other did not; Love benefited his team by stretching the floor while Rodman benefited his with DPOY level defense and toughness. Placing either one of them above the other in absolute terms is difficult, but most lists of historic greats such as the NBA's Top 75 will rank Rodman higher.

If Dwyane Wade was not your pick for LeBron James' most talented and impactful teammate, then it is likely Anthony Davis. The 6'10" Pelican migrated to Los Angeles to join LeBron and the Lakers in 2019, one year after LeBron landed there himself. Davis made himself known in the paint as a tremendous shot blocker and a skilled post to midrange scorer. He made a run at the Defensive Player of the Year award in several of his seasons leading up to his association with LeBron but never had the honor of taking first place in the voting. The same can be said of his MVP cases, finishing in the top 5 twice in 2015 (5th) and 2018 (3rd) but never climbing the ladder high enough to receive the trophy. In the year he traveled to "The Bubble" and won a championship with LeBron, Anthony Davis averaged 26.1 points, 9.3 rebounds, 3.2 assists, 1.5 steals, and 2.3 blocks. These are strong numbers, but the acclaim on that Laker team ends there. Aside from James and Davis, there was no one on the squad who made an All-Star team or All NBA team; there was no one considered for any individual awards (save an aged Dwight Howard down at 9th place in 6MOY); there was only one player who averaged double digit points in Kyle Kuzma at 12.8 (Dion Waiters technically did also but only played 7 games for Los Angeles); on top of all that, the roster had an average age of 28.1, the oldest in the NBA that year.

The primary thrust of the above paragraphs goes to show how spurious the claims of LeBron's "super teams" really are. Did James play alongside All-Star talent? He surely did. But the majority of his playing and winning did not occur with stacked rosters and the various players of renown he had occasion to team up with did not generally occur at the same time. But much like the discussion of the so called "clutch gene," it may not be in the simple reality of the facts that the fuel for LeBron's polemicists is found but rather in their attitudes about the surrounding situation. The fact of a "super team" is not what most

Jordan proponents really dislike, evinced by the fact that they rarely deride Magic, Kareem, and Worthy for being on the same team nor do they do so for Shaq and Kobe. The difference here is a perception of honor or regard for competition. Superb teams who are grown organically through draft picks or trades early in one's career are held in high esteem by these same ridiculers. A negative light is only brought upon LeBron for playing with other stars because of the perception that he moved their deliberately to do so. On its face, this can seem to make sense; in all games of sport it is the journey toward the goal that really inspires one with admiration, and therefore if something occurs to undermine that journey, the reward will be consequentially lessened. This is well demonstrated in championship runs like the Milwaukee Bucks in 2021 and the Golden State Warriors in 2022 where the weight of the world was placed upon the shoulders of a man (Giannis and Curry) who pushed through against the odds to deliver a win and complete a fairytale story for an underwhelming team or a long-starved franchise. But LeBron is not without this type of storyline himself. The 2016 championship was as much a fulfillment of duty to one's original team and storybook finish as the NBA has ever seen. And nowhere in the career of Michael Jordan was a single championship as hard earned as that one. Indeed, for the likes of Jordan, Magic, Kareem, Duncan, Kobe, Shaq, and many others who were drafted by or traded early enough to teams with other stars or superb construction around them, the capacity for such a storybook finish is off the table. These men were expected to win because their teams, their organizations, were great. One who is born into wealth is denied the opportunity to show the world he can pull himself up by his bootstraps. This, in a twisted way is unfortunate for him for it is his good fortune that holds him back in this regard. But none of these players chose where they would be drafted. They could not help it that they had little to no opportunity to play for an organization that needed them to single-handedly lift them to victory. And because they never had the need to search elsewhere for the requisite competence to win, they never did. But this cannot then be portrayed as a virtue. In the same way that a born aristocrat need not uproot his life to find wealth, players like Jordan who were drafted into organizations who drafted other stars like Pippen and then traded for others like Rodman had no need to try to improve their station by moving to another team. Those who criticize LeBron for moving to Miami to find a winning culture often neglect to criticize Jordan for being born with the sports equivalent of a silver spoon in the mouth. Were Jordan to have been drafted into different circumstances, he may have also opted to find a way out of his first team to chase a realistic chance of winning. This is another area of contemplation that is left largely up to the realm of speculation, but one interesting claim about the situation was recently made by NBA All-Star Gilbert Arenas. The former Washington Wizard now podcaster spoke on rumors that the Celtics thought of dealing Larry Bird away in the 1980's saying, "I got articles from when Boston was trying to trade Larry Bird to the Bulls. Jordan Said he'd take a pay cut. 'I can't beat him, I'll take a pay cut for him to come over here.' Most people can't get the print. I'm having editors from the 80's send me all their print work." He went on to say how Jordan claimed that he made enough money on outside endorsements to not worry about taking a pay cut if that's what it took to get Larry Legend on his team. If such claims have truth to them then this shifts the tone of Jordan's team construction from one of a man lucky enough to be drafted onto a team able to surround him with a winning makeup toward one of a man who was willing to do most anything to assemble the best possible squad. For those who rely on accusing LeBron of winning the wrong way in order to discredit his GOAT case, this blow to the aura of Michael Jordan as the ultimate competitor would surely sting.

Lastly, in the discussion of illustrious teammates, there must be a note made about Luka Doncic. In the wake of LeBron's twenty-second year, there is likely to be a storm of polemicists critiquing James for this most recent season as the Lakers made an unsatisfying round one exit from the playoffs despite the efforts of their two stars. LeBron cannot be criticized for riding the coattails of another great toward victory since Los Angeles did not win anything with this duo at the helm, but there's no doubt that murmurings will be made that LeBron *should have* won the title in 2025 if he had another top five player at his side. In response to this, one need only put that disappointing Timberwolves/Lakers series, as well as the season, in context.

The acquisition of Luka Doncic was as big a shock to the sports world as has been seen for decades. For days and weeks after the young Slovenian was traded, television and internet commentary all but revolved on the story. The Mavericks motivations, the baffling returns to Dallas, and the implications for the two teams and the league were all questioned endlessly when it was revealed that Luka would be swapped with Anthony Davis, the veteran Los Angeles center. Despite Davis' overall talent, this seemed to be an enormously lopsided trade in the Lakers favor primarily due to the ages of the two men in question. Doncic, now twenty-six, has the majority of his career and prime years still ahead of him while, if historic trends are to continue, Anthony Davis at thirty-two years old is closing in on end of his most productive years. The effect of this is that Los Angeles was able to set up the foundational piece for their next decade of basketball with the small price of that year's roster construction. With the loss of Anthony Davis, the Lakers instantly became a team in desperate need of size. Davis had been the defensive anchor of their squad, and with his departure, Los Angeles was left with only Jaxon Hayes, a raw, twenty-four year old to man the paint. When playoff time came coach JJ Redick saw that Hayes was not yet ready for the moment and Los Angeles was forced to play small ball with LeBron James as the tallest Laker on the court. The mismatched series against the Timberwolves was rife with schematic trouble as the Lakers scrambled to find answers to their lack of size. This included a second half of game four where the same five men played the entirety of the twenty-four minutes for the first time in NBA playoff history since those stats began recording in 1997. The series finished with another anomalous happening that perfectly demonstrated the problem with the Lakers roster. Rudy Gobert, notable for his four Defensive Player of the Year trophies, was instead the offensive engine for Minnesota in game five. Gobert recorded his playoff career high in points with 27 as well as reining in 24 rebounds. With respect to Gobert's abilities, the historic performance he put up was more of an indictment on the Lakers' inability to field anyone for the center position. All series long, Minnesota dominated the glass, outrebounding Los Angeles with bigger players and a fresher, deeper bench. And as was seen by the Lakers coaching staff, there are no schematic plans that stretch the height of your players half a foot to help contend at the rim. The lesson of this 2025 playoffs for all who watched it is one that was already known by those intimately involved with the game: roster construction is just as impactful as talent, and when the Lakers decided to trade their only inside presence away for the extended years of Doncic they understood that it likely meant a sacrifice of 2025's chances.

It is true that LeBron James played alongside a higher number of talented teammates. But the "super team" accusations toward James seem to fall flat when the numbers from those supporting casts are judged against the numbers of Jordan's teammates. There are individual instances where one of LeBron's second-in-commands outdid Jordan's Robin (Scottie Pippen) in a stat or two, but by and large Pippen had better production than those accused "super team" pieces. Some might raise issue by pointing to the production of a man like Anthony Davis who scored and rebounded at a high clip. This is true, but the Lakers team Anthony Davis played with LeBron on was never regarded as a "super team" as expectations fell away from LeBron as he aged and Davis had never proved himself to be a driving force for winning basketball prior to playing next to the King.

The second piece of the puzzle elucidated here is that LeBron's talented teammates are scattered. The four most productive men he suited up with are Wade, Irving, Davis, and Doncic, none of whom ever played alongside any of the others. What we find is that, contrary to the idea that LeBron needed a "super team" to win, James has done far more to prove that he can win no matter the situation than Jordan ever did. All of Michael's winning occurred in the same organization with much of the same team makeup around him. LeBron, on the other hand, has had to adapt en route to winning beside a shooting guard in Wade, a point guard in Irving, a big man in Davis, and a heliocentric figure in Doncic. This adaptation also occurs with a general absence of strong coaching, leading us only to conclude that the most important common denominator is LeBron himself.

12.
Sub-par Rosters

So far we have only investigated the positives of each man's teams; those things that helped him win a ring. But that is only half of the puzzle. There is a lot of NBA season that happens before the crowning of a champion, and therefore there is some degree of gradient to judging the idea of winning. For Jordan, things are simple because the vast majority of his seasons were either defined by a trophy or an unspectacular and early playoff exit. On the part of LeBron, there is more to the story. His six Finals losses mean that rather than lose early on in the playoffs like Michael Jordan was wont to do, there were half a dozen times where James was just a single step away from another championship. To understand how we should evaluate his ability to win, at least a brief inquiry needs to be made into a couple of these teams. Both the 2011 and 2014 team were made up largely of a Heat roster already examined, and another chunk of his appearances came with a Kyrie Irving and Kevin Love backed Cleveland squad in the years around the 2016 championship win. To illustrate the kind of load LeBron sometimes had to shoulder, we will delve into two of those other seasons where the King just barely missed out on gold.

The first and most widely discussed of his lackluster casts came in 2007. It was LeBron's first entrance into the Finals, a feat which he had accomplished at the age of only 22 (Jordan didn't make his first Finals until he was 28). Stepping onto that stage beside him was a list of names you might only remember if you grew up cheering for LeBron in the mid-2000's: Drew Gooden, Larry Hughes, Zydrunas Ilgauskas, Sasha Pavlovic, Daniel Gibson, Anderson Varejão, Damon Jones, Donyell Marshall, Eric Snow, David Wesley, Shannon Brown, Ira Newble, Dwayne Jones, and Scot Pollard. The lack of name recognition alone might drive one to consider this team a surprising contender for the NBA title. By Five-Thirty-Eight's estimation, this is not only a woefully bad Finals team but a historically bad one. In their all time ranking of supporting casts to make it to the last series of the year, these 2007 Cavaliers rank second to last. If that weren't bad enough, early in the series, Larry Hughes went down with a torn plantar fascia which caused him to miss half the games. Hughes was Cleveland's second highest contributor throughout the season with his average of 14.9 points, 3.8 rebounds, and 3.7 assists. As mediocre as these numbers are, it was the most help LeBron James had that year, and without even the assistance of Larry Hughes, there was little hope for that team no matter who led them.

One would hope the 2007 Finals was as bad as things got for LeBron when it comes to supporting casts. Arguably, it was, but it is an argument. The other ignominious candidate for such a spot is that of the last year of his second stint in Cleveland.

The 2018 Cavaliers might appear great on paper. One looking up a roster will find All-Star names like Dwayne Wade, Kyle Korver, Derrick Rose, Kyrie Irving and Kevin Love. But these stars were not able to make an on-court impact in the way their names might suggest. Due to age, injury, or both, not one of the once capable backcourt stars of Kyrie, Wade, and Rose were able to log even a single minute of play time in the Finals. And while the team did have some competent shooters in Kevin Love and Kyle Korver, the loss of their guards forced other players into playmaking roles that they were ill-suited for. Aside from LeBron James, the 2018 Cavaliers had virtually no one who could get the offense moving and create an open shot. This is reflected in the fact that LeBron's 40 assists in the series almost outdid the 44 recorded by the rest of the team combined. LeBron also scored a full third of Cleveland's points (136 out of 410) by averaging 34.0. And if it can be believed, the offensive side of the ball is where those Cavs were comparatively good. Throughout that 2017-18 season, Cleveland ranked second to last in the NBA in defensive rating with 111.1, a mark that is so far the worst of all time for any team that made it to the Finals.

Whichever team you decide to pick as the worst supporting cast behind LeBron is up to your own subjective distaste, but deciding between them is really not the point here. What needs to be kept in focus is that, aside from 2011, LeBron's losses in the Finals are not due to any conceivable failure on his part. The teams he found himself on were continually overmatched by their opponents; even the once dominant Heatles aged to a point where the supporting cast of 2014 was ranked in Five-Thirty-Eight's list as the eighth worst of all time. Michael Jordan never had such an incapable crew around him. In fact, in that same set of rankings, Jordan's 1996 Bulls top the list for best supporting cast of all time. The 1997 and 1998 teams also both come in the top six. So while it is true to say that Jordan won all of the six Finals he made an appearance in, it may be more truthful to say that *the Chicago Bulls* won those championships.

It was demonstrated earlier how the strength of the Bulls' team hardly suffered when Jordan was away as they won only two fewer games the year he took off to play baseball. Since we're in the midst of such team strength comparisons, now would be a perfect time to take a quick look at what happened to the teams LeBron James was the engine for once he decided to leave.

The first of these teams is the recently described 2000's Cavaliers. The roster construction was a bit different in 2010 when LeBron decided to take his talents to

South Beach. Cleveland had gone 61-21 that season en route to a second round playoff fight against the Boston Celtics. The next season came, and without LeBron those same Cavaliers flipped the entire way around by winning just 19 games and losing 63. The loss of the King swung Cleveland from the first seed in the Eastern Conference the year before all the way down to very last place in 2011.

But the Cavaliers had little star power to potentially captain the ship, an understandable reason for collapse. This should mean that the Miami Heat, still then the home of Dwyane Wade and Chris Bosh, would be just fine if they happened to lose a third star in LeBron James, right? Again, we can see LeBron's impact as the Heat fell from 54-28 the year before he left down to 37-45 without him. Miami also suffered a precipitous fall in the regular season standings going from second down to tenth.

Two instances of franchise collapse after the departure of LeBron would be interesting, but three would be an irrefutable pattern. Our third case study occurs back in Cleveland two seasons after LeBron delivered on his promise to bring a title to his home state. Those 2018 Cavaliers (the same team whose faults were discussed above) went 50-32 with LeBron around but fell to 19-63 without him in 2019.

In summation of all the names the last three chapters have supplied, the superstars in their primes, the superstars past their primes, the successful role players, and the small contributors who we tend to forget, a demonstration can be made of how much help either Jordan or LeBron had by pointing out that the number of playoff wins Michael Jordan pulled off without a teammate who made an All-Star, All NBA, or All Defensive team that year is fourteen. LeBron James nearly quadruples that total with fifty-five wins. So while some critics of LeBron will attempt to use the idea that he played alongside many fellow hall of famers as evidence of the assistance he needed, the truth could not be further away. When we put all of those names in context we see that the vast majority of the time it was Michael who had the best in the league on his side.

What we have seen in this chapter echoes a similar counter-narrative strand to that of the chapter examining the meaning of clutch. Despite the cascade of criticism hurled upon LeBron for doing all of his winning as part of "super teams," the facts are again nearly opposite. While James has played alongside other special talents, those players have achieved very little in the realm of accolades without the King leading their team. And when we dive into any inquiry beyond mere talent of the supposed stars, such as coaching or roster construction, LeBron has been among the least fortunate players ever.

13.
Strength of Opposition

The strength of one's own team cannot be sufficiently placed into context until we scrutinize the opposite side of that coin: who is that team playing against? The opposition, after all, plays as large a part in who wins a game as the subject does.

If an NBA team were to go undefeated but we learned later that they played an entire season against a gaggle of fifth graders, we obviously wouldn't put any stock in their success. No one denies that the better an opposition is the more impressive it is for them to be defeated. In the realm of ideas, we can agree there. In practice, however, we don't have a simple method of grading the teams our GOAT candidates played against. But what we do have is several methods that can speak to different aspects of those contemporary competitions, and by a patchwork of information, we can come to a solid understanding of how impressive the relative success was.

We might start simple by picking a small sample of important games that often get discussed; each man's Finals appearances. To get an immediate understanding of the teams who faced off against each other in these sixteen Finals, we can look back at the betting favorites and underdogs. Las Vegas line setters certainly can't claim to be the sole arbiters of truth in sports, but they are typically people whose livelihoods require them to be consistently accurate in predicting competition outcomes and therefore show no favoritism due to personal feelings. People unfamiliar with the language of gambling may find the sight of such figures confusing, but even without delving into the mathematical nitty gritty, the story they tell will be easy to understand.

LeBron	Finals Odds	Win Probability
2007	+360	21.74%
2011	-175	63.64%
2012	+155	39.22%
2013	-220	68.75%
2014	+135	42.55%
2015	+190	34.48%
2016	+180	35.71%
2017	+250	28.57%
2018	+688	12.69%
2020	-350	77.78%

Jordan	Finals Odds	Win Probability
1991	-200	66.67%
1992	-250	71.43%
1993	-240	70.59%
1996	-950	90.48%
1997	-600	85.71%
1998	-115	53.49%

For the entirely uninitiated, the easiest way to explain the betting numbers is to say that if the odds number is negative, then that team is favored to win and if the odds number is positive, it means that team is the underdog. The larger that number (in either the positive or negative direction) the more emphatically they are expected to win or lose. As one can see at a glance, Michael Jordan's Bulls were favored in every single Finals series he played in. One might attempt to make the argument that they were favored by so much because Jordan was the best player in the series, but that logic fails after even a cursory exploration of team sports. Having the best player in a series certainly helps your chances, but in team sports where there are so many variables involved, one player cannot make the entire difference. Take the 2021 Finals for instance where it was the Phoenix Suns who were favored over the Bucks despite the fact that Milwaukee had the consensus best player in back to back MVP Giannis Antetokounmpo. The reason for the Bulls' constant high regard is best explained in the section on *Jordan's Team Strength*.

While the Bulls always walked in the door with the upper hand, the numbers for LeBron James' Finals teams look quite different. Despite being undisputedly the best player, of the ten Finals series LeBron has been to, he's only been the betting favorite three times. Those seven other times he was named as the underdog.

Now that we have a general overview of what LeBron and Jordan's championship scenarios were, we can take a closer look at some of the teams they played against in those games. In order to illustrate the strength of those players and teams, a variety of factors will be considered such as statistical performances, personal awards, strong consideration for personal awards, and others. One way we can get a glimpse at how good each man's opponents were is by seeing where those men rank against each other. Of course, there is no objective ranking, but during the NBA's 75th anniversary year, the league came out with a list of its own creation to order these legends. It is not a perfect list since it was composed in 2021 and therefore had no way of considering the remainder of the careers for any still active players. This means that most of the players LeBron James played against will have the opportunity to move up this list as their legacy grows and what is written here may indeed undervalue them in the end. With that said, we shall indicate where any individual player landed on this list with their respective placement in parentheses (#X) after the first mention of their name.

In his six Finals appearances, Michael Jordan played

against the Los Angeles Lakers, the Portland Trailblazers, the Phoenix Suns, The Seattle SuperSonics, and twice against the Utah Jazz.

That first championship in 1991 showcased a Lakers team with some big names like Magic Johnson (#4), James Worthy (#56), and Byron Scott. This particular series, however, is fraught with issues. This was the last season Magic Johnson played before receiving his diagnosis as HIV positive. We do not mean to claim the disease had a significantly negative impact on his play or that it was even present in his body then, but the historical moment ought to be noted. As for James Worthy, on the other hand, there is a more pertinent story. It happened that in the preceding series where the Lakers battled the Portland Trailblazers, Worthy came down with an awkward landing that sprained his left ankle. He played through the injury with clear limitations that got even worse when the same ankle was reinjured in the very first game of the Finals against Chicago. Big Game James continued to fight it out, but his restrictions were an awful handicap for the Lakers as he was both their leading scorer that year as well as the man who was supposed to be tasked with guarding Michael Jordan. The other key piece for the Lakers, Byron Scott, was also riddled with injury problems as he suffered a reaggravation of his hamstring during that 1991 Finals. Scott had hurt the same muscle two seasons beforehand, and such repeated injuries eventually caused his NBA decline. The takeaway from all this is that while on its face it seems Jordan's 1991 ring came against a cast of strong opponents, it was unfortunately a hobbled version of those men and a lone Magic Johnson attempting to rework the cohesion of a broken team on the spot.

In the 1992 Finals, the only really noteworthy member of the Trailblazers was Clyde Drexler (#53). While he was a wonderful player in the day and age, from history's perspective, Drexler was only a one time champion (1995) and the highest individual honor he claimed was a single appearance on the All NBA First Team roster.

The 1993 Finals share a similar problem to the first of Jordan's championships. While there was a memorable player on the opposition, there was only the one in Charles Barkley (#22). Barkley was fantastic that year and won the 1993 MVP but never won a championship for himself despite individual dominance.

1996 was the matchup against the Seattle Supersonics, a team that featured a few nice players, but none in the top echelon of NBA names. Gary Payton (#42), Shawn Kemp, and Detlef Schrempf led that team, averaging 19.3, 19.6, and 17.1 points respectively. Despite their success in the regular season, this Seattle team's roster was looked upon as such an outmatched competitor for the Bulls that Bob Costas could be heard uttering these words of the upcoming Finals: "With due respect to the Seattle Supersonics and apologies to their fans, the prevailing attitude in Chicago and through most of the country really is that these NBA Finals loom not so much as a competition as a coronation. This is viewed as the greatest mismatch in NBA Finals history."

In 1997, Chicago had their first of back to back matchups against the Utah Jazz. As far as big names go, the Jazz feature two in Karl Malone (#23) and John Stockton (#24). This Utah duo proved to be a lethal pair for much of their respective careers, though it has to be noted that when Jordan finally met and beat them in these championship games Malone was already thirty-three years old and Stockton was thirty-four. The next year not much had changed for the Utah roster except for the fact that Malone and Stockton had gotten yet another year older. Whether it was age or another factor, this Jazz team combined for one of the worst NBA Finals appearances ever, scoring just 54 total points in Game 3 after racking up 26 turnovers. To his credit, Karl Malone, advanced in age as he was, had won the MVP in 1998 and still averaged 25.0 points and 10.5 rebounds. However, with his partner in crime already so aged (averaging only single digit points and 8.7 assists that series), this rounds out a neat pattern we see in Jordan's Finals opponents; that being in every Finals he was a part of, the Bulls did face one great player, but never multiple at a time without a serious asterisk.

LeBron James' Finals appearances look starkly different. In 2007 LeBron made his first trip to that last series of the NBA season where his Cavaliers found themselves looking across the court at the San Antonio Spurs. The Spurs were led then, as they were for the next decade, by the great Tim Duncan (#8). Duncan took 4th in MVP voting that year while simultaneously being 3rd in DPOY. Few need explanation of how good a player Tim Duncan was, but some will forget Tony Parker, the point guard of the team. Parker was an All-Star that year along with Duncan, but the team's talent didn't stop there. Coming off the sideline for the Spurs was perhaps the greatest bench player in basketball's long history: Manu Ginobili. Ginobili, who would unquestionably have been a starter on most teams but took the position of lower status in order to create the most optimal rotation for the Spurs, was runner-up in 2007 6th Man of the Year voting. We're also compelled to point out that Bruce Bowen, the Spurs small forward, was the runner-up for DPOY, finishing one spot ahead of Duncan. Lastly, a San Antonio team cannot be passed by without mentioning the fact that they were coached by Gregg Popovich. The revered "Pop" has had a career envied by almost everyone as his continuous success has led him to take the mantel as the coach with the most wins in NBA history.

The next time LeBron James made it to the Finals was 2011, his first year in Miami. This is the biggest blemish on LeBron's career. It was a series where he most objectively did not play up to his standards. That being said, the star player on the other side of the court was Dallas' Dirk Nowitzki (#17). The Maverick legend was a perennial All-Star and landed all the way up at No. 17 on the NBA's Top

75 list. At point guard, the Mavericks had another of all time greats in Jason Kidd (#43), though it must be noted that Kidd was, despite his surname, reaching the end of his career and was one of the older players in the league then. But just as the 2007 Spurs had a formidable defender and a spectacular bench leader on their squad, the Mavericks started Tyson Chandler at center who was 3rd in DPOY voting and Jason Terry, the runner-up for 6MOY. That lackluster 2011 performance from LeBron, though disappointing, turned into the start of true playoff dominance as it would fuel a run of eight consecutive Finals.

2012 bring us to the year of LeBron's first championship win. It came against the Oklahoma City Thunder who, while young, sported one of the most talented cores in NBA history. The Thunder were led by Kevin Durant (#12) who averaged 28.0 points per game and was runner-up in the season's MVP race. But Durant was not the only MVP candidate from OKC that year. Their star point guard, Russell Westbrook (#68) also received consideration as he finished 12th in total MVP voting to round out his All-Star season. As talented as these Thunder leaders were in their starting roles, the team hardly took a decline when they went to the bench since they also employed the 6th Man of the Year winner in James Harden (#50), a man who had yet to fully hone his capabilities but would go on to become one of the most prolific scorers and passers the league has ever seen. And if all of that talent weren't enough to make a formidable team, the Thunder were anchored by Serge Ibaka who took 2nd place overall in the Defensive Player of the Year selection.

The next season LeBron completed his back-to-back championships with some vengeance for his first appearance in 2007. This 2013 rematch against the Spurs included all of the names, save for Bruce Bowen, listed above, but in addition, San Antonio had added another key piece of talent in Kawhi Leonard (#33).

The following season featured LeBron's third matchup with the San Antonio dynasty. This 2014 Spurs team had all the same parts as the previous year along with an even more well-developed bench with three of those players receiving consideration for 6th Man of the Year (Manu Ginobili, Marco Belinelli, and Patty Mills).

2015 starts a run unlike many seen in the history of sports. The next four consecutive championships would feature LeBron's Cleveland Cavaliers and the Golden State Warriors. The Warriors had a few slight, and one extreme, changes to their team composition, but the core all started with Steph Curry (#16). Little if any evidence is needed to support the claim that Curry is, to this day, the best shooter to ever touch a basketball. His offensive gravity can hardly be overstated. In addition to rewriting the entire record book on three-point shots, Curry also sits very near the top of the NBA's all time rankings for *true shooting percentage*, a stat that is usually dominated by big men like Rudy Gobert and DeAndre Jordan because of their routine looks near the rim. Aside from the historical respect that Curry has garnered, it must be remembered that he also won the 2015 MVP award en route to the Finals. And as good of a shooter as Steph Curry was, he was not the only distance threat to keep an eye on. Klay Thompson, also on the short list of shooting GOATs, was named to an All-Star game that year as well as placing 10th in MVP voting due to his tremendous play. Any team would be hard pressed to compete against a squad with this much offensive firepower, but on top of that, the Warriors did not lack for impactful names on the defensive end as well. Draymond Green took 2nd in the race for Defensive Player of the Year while his teammate Andrew Bogut placed 6th. And much like the Spurs before them, Golden State had a depth that could hold their own against most starters in the league as multiple Warriors finished with good consideration for the 6MOY award (Andre Iguodala and Marreese Speights).

As strong as that Golden State team was, the 2016 Warriors went to a place of achievement untouched by any

NBA greats. The crew finished their regular season with an astonishing 73 wins and 9 losses. This remains the best regular season record in NBA history, and with a horde of individual honors to go along with it, it's not difficult to see why. Steph Curry led the league in scoring and won his second MVP in a row, this time by unanimous decision (the first player to ever achieve such acclaim). Klay Thompson made another trip to the All-Star game as did teammate Draymond Green. Green also repeated his placement of runner-up in DPOY selection and even took 7th overall in the deliberation for MVP. The Warriors lost no depth on the team either as both Andre Iguodala and Shaun Livingston received votes for 6MOY (2nd and 11th respectively). Despite being quite arguably the greatest team of all time up until then, LeBron and the Cavs made their historic comeback from down 3 games to 1 in the NBA Finals, giving LeBron his third ring.

Then, unbelievably, the Warriors upgraded yet again. After their Finals loss to LeBron's Cavaliers, Golden State recruited Kevin Durant, one of the league's top talents. It is contended by many that these 2017 Warriors were the single greatest basketball team ever assembled. The prowess of Steph Curry, Klay Thompson, and Draymond Green has already been described, but it should be noted that the trio had not fallen off from dominant play. All three were All-Star selections again, Curry was 6th in MVP voting, and Green had summitted the mountain and earned his first DPOY trophy. Added to this dominant core is a fourth All-Star in Kevin Durant who also had MVP votes cast his way. On top of all of this, Andre Iguodala remained a constant contributor from the bench which made him runner-up for 6MOY.

Not much changed in the following year of 2018. Again LeBron met the Warriors in the Finals and again their core of four was together. Each of those four Warriors stars was elected to the All-Star team with both Durant and Curry receiving more votes for MVP. It must not be lost in all the highlights and raining three-point shots that though this group was a historic offensive explosion, they were also an elite defensive team. Green, Durant, and Thompson were each considered for Defensive Player of the Year in 2018, landing in 6th, 9th, and 11th respectively.

After that onslaught of Spurs and Warriors match-ups, LeBron James played his tenth NBA Finals against his former franchise, the Miami Heat, in 2020. This is undoubtedly the opponent with the least amount of historic stature when it comes to the individual players. Though they had two All-Stars in Jimmy Butler and Bam Adebayo, the 2020 Heat made it to the championship primarily due to their strength in close games as well as an impressive depth with eight different players averaging double digit points for them that season.

There we have it; sixteen opposing teams over the years of James and Jordan's Finals appearances. It's a lot to take in, so we shall collect a few sets of facts to compare things side by side. First, if we take the NBA's 75th anniversary team as an indication of how great a player was, we can see that LeBron played against more of the greats than Jordan did (nine to eight). And while Michael played against several big names, when it comes to the best of the best, say the top twenty players of all time, Jordan only played against one of them in the Finals (Magic Johnson) whereas LeBron played against four (Dirk Nowitzki, Steph Curry, Kevin Durant, and Tim Duncan, three of which he had to play against multiple times).

Narrowing down to the individual honors of those specific years we see that Jordan and LeBron each played against the current MVP twice. But the eye-popping difference here comes in the defenders they had to play against. In Jordan's Finals, he played against just two opponents who finished in the top five for Defensive Player of the Year that season; LeBron, on the other hand, played against eight. Some may argue that happened because LeBron played in four more Finals than Jordan did, but even if we bring James down to six Finals by stripping him of the 2013, 2014, 2018, and 2020 appearances, this number of great defenders is still two to seven in LeBron's favor.

Finals opponents who finished top 5 in DPOY voting that year.

Jordan	LeBron
Gary Payton 1st	Tim Duncan 3rd
Dan Majerle 5th	Bruce Bowen 2nd
	Tyson Chandler 3rd
	Serge Ibaka 2nd
	Draymond Green 2nd
	Draymond Green 2nd
	Draymond Green 1st
	Bam Adebayo 5th

Furthermore, we can look at the team construction of their opponents. A pattern was elucidated earlier showing how Jordan's Finals opponents feature a single great player, but never a collection of great players who weren't injured or past their primes. This is with the possible exception of Stockton and Malone in 1997 and 1998 as Karl Malone was still garnering MVP consideration despite his age; though his partner John Stockton, on the other hand, was not at that same level in these years likely due to being in his mid-thirties. LeBron's opponents do not share this pattern. There are some similar individual cases such as Dirk's Dallas Mavericks in 2011, but by and large, LeBron was going up against dynastic collections of great players with the Spurs and Golden State Warriors.

Despite the necessary variance that ten Finals appearances will have, LeBron's losses cannot be laid solely, or even largely, at his feet when one sees that his Finals numbers are remarkably similar in virtually every category regardless of whether he won or lost that series.

LeBron Average Stats in 4 Finals Wins and 6 Finals Losses

	Pts	Reb	Ast	Stl	Blk	FG%	3PT%	FT%	TS%
Wins	28.3	11.1	8.0	2.0	1.1	49.7	35.5	75.3	57.6
Losses	28.5	9.5	7.7	1.5	0.6	47.3	34.9	71.4	55.3

Some will attempt to dismiss these facts by saying that it is not a player's fault who he has to play against; you play who is in front of you and do your best to win. While there is an element of truth to this sentiment, there is another ethic that it misses out on. Much of the glory of sport has to do with performing well on the biggest stage, and who you beat is an integral part of that equation. Jordan fans implicitly believe this when citing his six championship rings as evidence of GOAT status since there is another man with nearly double that. Bill Russell, the legendary Celtic, has eleven NBA titles to his name. When this comparison arises, Russell's accomplishments are usually belittled in pro-Jordan minds because the standard of competition was not as stringent in those days as it was later on. There were fewer teams and fewer great players back then. But if this fact can dampen the significance of Bill Russell's championships, why wouldn't it do the same when comparing Jordan's to LeBron's? Of course, it should and it does. There is no objective math to say precisely how much more impressive LeBron's titles were than Jordan's, but in the spirit of honest comparison, we have to acknowledge the fact that LeBron played and beat much stronger competition.

And this difference in the quality of their wins is not without chances afforded to Jordan. Though it was not in the Finals, Michael too faced off against some dynastic greats in Larry Bird's Celtics and the Bad Boy Pistons under the leadership of Isiah Thomas. In his long career against those two players (Bird, Thomas) Jordan was a measly 22-53 in both the regular season and playoffs; when it comes to playoff series against them Michael went just 1-5.

PEAK AND LONGEVITY

14.
Definition 1

The response to LeBron's continued playoff success (and wrapped up inside the "6-0" discussion) is the claim that Michael Jordan is the GOAT because he had the highest peak performance of any player ever. This is another claim filled with assumptions that may vary depending on who happens to be making the assertion. *Peak* may be an integrally important aspect of a player's overall greatness, but there is no standard definition of what it means. Some aspects of play can be recorded by hard stats while others that might contribute to one's best version of themselves are less tangible and therefore immeasurable. And secondly, even after we determine a set of statistics or separate metrics that might measure one's peak, what duration of time are we talking about? Is it a single moment? A single game? Perhaps it is a month or a season. Maybe two or three seasons cover enough ground to be a fair definition. More still could be argued since in topographical terms the higher a mountain climbs the wider it tends to stretch as well. And if a so-called peak is maintained for a longer amount of time, is it worth more than a briefer peak of similar height? There is simply no consensus.

No one is likely to claim a peak definition that encompasses only a single play, and if they were to do so they ought to refer back to the *Clutch* section where such things are examined. Widening out from there, we might look to a player's single best game of all time. If we're looking for the game each man played to the best of his abilities we may find difficulty in lining up the statistics and weighing their importance properly, so in the spirit of conservatism and graciousness, we shall lean toward Michael Jordan's specialty of scoring. This stat will provide a simple enough metric for comparison.

Jordan's highest scoring game of all time came in a 1990 battle against the Cavaliers. He scored 69 points in that Cleveland thriller. LeBron James had his highest scoring game during his last season with the Heat. He put up 61 points against Charlotte shortly before the arrival of the 2014 playoffs. Judging strictly on this point total it would seem that Jordan had the higher peak. That is, until you notice that the Bulls' contest with the Cavs that day went into overtime, causing Jordan to play an inflated minute count of 50. LeBron, on the other hand, only got to play for 41 minutes as his highest scoring game ended in regulation. This isn't exactly comparing apples to apples, and if we adjust LeBron's points scored based on the number of minutes Michael played (50), we see that James' performance was proportional to scoring 74 points in a 50 minute overtime game. If the reader thinks this type of math is too presumptive to count a point toward LeBron, we might take Michael's second highest scoring game of all time (one that actually ended in regulation). This was a 1993 meeting with the Orlando Magic where Jordan scored 64 points. Again, at first glance, it seems irrational to say this higher score was worse than LeBron's 61 until one has a closer look at the box score. First it should be noted that the Bulls lost this game, and that again Jordan played a significantly higher amount of time with 47 minutes played compared to LeBron's 41. But that is not the smoking gun. The story of this game comes down to the fact that Jordan attempted an astounding 49 shots in order to make it to this point total. In contrast, in LeBron's 61 point performance, he took just 33 attempts. That's right, in their best regulation games ever, Jordan outscored LeBron by 3 points, but it took him 16 extra shots to do it. This situation is all too emblematic of the discrepancy between LeBron James' and Michael Jordan's scoring efficiencies.

15.
Definition 2

Many will reasonably reject the idea that the last section's parameters of one game can define a man's *peak*. In response, we should expand our lens a bit more. Picking any particular portion of a season may seem arbitrary, so let's venture into a metric whose duration is dependent on success; winning streaks. The 1995-96 season is where Michael Jordan's Bulls had their most dominant single stretch of games after winning 18 in a row. This is good enough to tie the 2022 Suns, the 2020 Bucks, the 1982 Celtics, and the 1970 Knicks for the 10th longest streak ever. It is an impressive feat, but pales in comparison to LeBron James' longest winning streak of 27 games. This occurred in the 2012-13 season en route to his second championship and is currently in the slot of 2nd for longest streaks in NBA history (beaten out only by the 1971-72 Lakers streak of 33).

But since winning is also a team stat it, we would be remiss to go without examining the production of each start within the bounds of those games to determine how influential they were to their organization's success. During Chicago's streak of 18 wins, Michael averaged 31.2 points, 3.8 assists, and 6.1 rebounds. In contrast, the Heat's 27 game win streak saw LeBron averaging 27.0 points, 8.0 assists, and 8.1 rebounds. Like most other situations between these two, Michael Jordan scored about four more points than LeBron but the King outdid the Jumpman in the other facets of the game. When one looks toward the fact that LeBron recorded more than double Jordan's assists it can be easily calculated (generously assuming only 2 points per assist) that LeBron and Jordan's total points generated for their offenses during these stretches were nearly identical. Combine that virtual tie with the fact that LeBron rebounded significantly better and has the long history of more accurate shooting percentages and it is plain to see that not only was LeBron's highest peak sustained for a larger number of games than Jordan's but he was also more productive toward his team's wins in those games.

So if the best single game goes to LeBron and the longest undefeated stretch of games goes to LeBron, what might we see if we look instead to an entire season?

16.
<u>Definition 3</u>

  Picking Michael Jordan's best season comes with a few obstacles. There is an early candidate in 1987-88 when Jordan won both the MVP and the DPOY awards. However, this year is tarnished by the fraudulency of the defensive stats discussed back in the chapter on defense as well as the fact that the Bulls did not win the NBA title that year and, in fact, only made it to the second round where they were nearly swept by the Pistons 1 game to 4. Naming a season without a title or really even any playoff success as Jordan's best year would be an obvious contradiction to the other most popular claim for his GOAT case (the "6-0" Finals record). The other candidate for Jordan's best season is likely to be named as that of 1990-91. This was the year he and the Bulls won their first championship in which Jordan finished the season averaging 31.5 points, 5.5 assists, 6.0 rebounds, 2.7 steals, and 1.0 blocks. To get an idea of his offensive efficiency that year, we can look at his shot attempts per game (22.4) alongside his field goal percentage of 53.9%. Jordan also won the MVP that season as well as being named to both the All-Star team and the All NBA First Team. He did not win DPOY but did earn some consideration as he took 7ᵗʰ overall in the voting.

  To compare, we shall take 2012-13 as the prime example of LeBron's best year. This was also a championship season for him and the Heat, the second of their back-to-back titles. James completed the season averaging 26.8 points, 7.3 assists, 8.0 rebounds, 1.7 steals, and 0.9 blocks. In accomplishing this, LeBron took just 17.8 field goal attempts per game while shooting 56.5%.

Like Jordan's best year, he was also awarded the MVP as well as named to the All-Star game and the All NBA First Team. Though James did not win the DPOY, he took 2nd place overall and very arguably should have won it due to the Marc Gasol controversy discussed in the *Defense* chapter.

At first look, one might award the best season to Michael's side as he scored almost 5 more points per game. However, like we saw routinely in the *Scoring* section, it is efficiency that tells the true tale. While Jordan averaged nearly 5 more total points, he also averaged nearly 5 more total shot attempts. Not only did he shoot more often than James, but he shot at a worse percentage. If one were to add 5 extra shots to James' games and assume his 56.5% success rate stayed constant, we would see that LeBron's point total per game would not only rival Jordan's but actually exceed it.

$$Jordan\ s\ FGAs\ (22.4) - Lebron\ s\ FGAs\ (17.8) = 4.6\ extra\ shots$$
$$4.6 \times 2\ (assuming\ only\ 2\ pt\ FGA) = 9.2\ possible\ points$$
$$9.2 \times 0.565\ (Lebron\ s\ FG\%) = 5.2\ extra\ points$$
$$5.2 + 26.8\ (Lebron\ s\ original\ points) = 32.0$$
$$32\ (LBJ\ per\ 22.4\ attempts) > 31.5\ (MJ\ per\ 22.4\ attempts)$$

This is in addition to the fact that he averaged nearly 2 full assists more than the Bulls star as well as 2 entire rebounds. All put together, we see that LeBron is scoring more effectively, assisting his teammates more often, securing more possessions both through more rebounds and fewer wasted shot attempts, and also getting significantly closer to being named Defensive Player of the Year. For the third metric in a row, the argument of peak is standing firmly on the side of LeBron James.

17.
Definition 4

Of course, the Jordan fan will likely attempt to dismiss these metrics as fallacious and insist that the true meaning of peak is shown in the fact of Jordan's three consecutive championships. Since this happened twice but there was a two year hiatus in between the events during which Jordan played little to no professional basketball at all, we must resist the insistence of some who would like to place phantom achievements that *would have* occurred during this time. We are then also forced to either pick one of the three-championship runs or include the entire eight year stretch together, a complexity that would drop Jordan's averages down quite a bit if he were to score zeros in so many categories. For all of these reasons, we shall pick just the run of championships that include the 1990-01, 1991-92, and 1992-93 seasons. This is done for a dual reason. First, it is because Jordan's personal statistics are on the whole higher in this run than they are in the second one of 1996-98. Secondly, because the later Bulls have a full roster of Jordan, Pippen, Rodman, Kerr, Kukoc, and others, most onlookers would consider this the more formidable version of the 90's Bulls and therefore we can give more credit to Jordan's peak if we pick the earlier run wherein he had less help toward success.

So what does the best three season stretch of Jordan's career look like statistically? Between the 1990-91 to 1992-93 seasons, Michael Jordan averaged 31.4 points, 5.7 assists, 6.4 rebounds, 2.6 steals, and 0.9 blocks. This was all done while shooting 51.8% from the floor and taking 23.6 shots per game (an average of 1.33 points per shot). He won 3 championships, 2 MVP awards, and was named to 3 All-Star games as well as 3 All NBA First Teams. His average DPOY placement over those years was 4th without winning one.

Conversely, LeBron's best three year stretch will go from the 2011-12 season through the 2013-14 season. His statistical averages were of 27.0 points, 6.6 assists, 7.6 rebounds, 1.7 steals, and 0.7 blocks. LeBron did this on 55.4% shooting while taking just 18.1 shots per game (an average of 1.49 points per shot). During this stretch, he won 2 NBA championships, 2 MVP awards, and was named to 3 All-Star games as well as 3 All NBA First Teams. His average DPOY placement was precisely the same as Jordan's (4th) but without the history of inflated defensive stats.

The places where LeBron beats Jordan can stand for themselves. Those categories where Jordan seems to outdo LeBron, on the other hand, may be misleading. The story is the same as we have seen in previous investigations: it is one of efficiency. While Jordan did score an average of 4.4 more points over their peak years, it took him 5.5 more shots to do it. Not only did he shoot significantly more but he shot significantly worse, 3.6% worse overall. When one corrects the amount of points each man is generating for their team based on how many of their team's shots they are using up, LeBron James not only meets Jordan but exceeds him in scoring. The comparative math looks like this. LeBron's average of 1.49 points per shot multiplied by an extra 5.5 field goal attempts (to equal him to Jordan's) would give him an estimated 8.2 extra points per game. Adding this to his current point total, we can see that if LeBron were to have taken as many shots as Jordan did, he would have blown him out of the water in scoring (LeBron: 35.2, Jordan: 31.4).

Once the scoring scales are evened, the only arguments Jordan's peak has a possible edge in are that of the defensive stats and the number of championships won. The defensive statistics are currently veiled in a certain amount of obscurity based on the Bulls' documented inflation of Michael Jordan's steals and blocks numbers. Unless a career long audit of these numbers is made alongside the tapes of the games, it is impossible to give an accurate assessment of them. One thing we can say with some type of solidity on the defensive front is that the two men during these peak stretches averaged the same placement in DPOY voting. This combined with Jordan's higher, but questionable stats, and LeBron's higher versatility leads us to conclude this messy category as close to a tie as we might be able to experience.

The final point of contention then is the championships. During LeBron's three year peak, he won two Larry O'Brien trophies. During Jordan's three year peak, he won three. This is clearly a point for the Jordan camp, though it isn't by much. While LeBron did not win a third championship in three years, he did make it to the NBA Finals in that third season. The Heat lost 1 game to 4 against the San Antonio Spurs, meaning that LeBron was only three games away from equaling Jordan in this peak category as well. They are, undeniably, important games with a heavy weight to them, but in order to believe that three individual games outweigh the dramatic leads LeBron has in scoring, assisting, and rebounding while everything else is essentially a wash, one must be the wearer of Bulls-colored glasses.

We could go on with a dozen more subjective definitions of what constitutes the true idea of *peak*. But we have already given several different meanings, each of which illustrates a vastly different type of dominance, and the same man has come out on top every single time. And all of this, dear reader, happened while judging the two primarily on scoring, a basis on which Jordan rests all his strengths. There was a large temptation to focus more on all of the other numbers (assists, rebounds, shooting percentages, etc.) that almost always lean LeBron's way by a large margin. But the amount of repetition in LeBron's obvious winning categories would have made for an entirely redundant read. We therefore went as charitable as could be asked with our choice of metric for a man's peak and continually came away with the same answer. There is little confidence left in the idea of searching for a basketball mountain where the flag of LeBron James is not currently planted at the summit.

18.
Longevity

There is virtually no area of the LeBron vs. Jordan debate that is less controversial than that surrounding longevity. The portions of previous chapters that focused on cumulative stats already illuminated much of this discussion, so in the interest of saving space for the reader's attention, a simple, cursory display will be made of those numbers.

	Points	Assists	Rebounds	Steals	Blocks	FG%	3P%
Jordan	32,292	5,633	6,672	2,514	893	49.7%	32.7%
LeBron	42,184	11,584	11,731	2,345	1,150	50.6%	34.9%

There are at least two important dimensions up for discussion when examining longevity. The first is quite straightforward: the duration of one's career. It is often said in sports that the best ability is availability as one simply cannot contribute toward winning if they aren't there in the first place. This encompasses both the breadth of one's career, that is, how many years there were from start to finish, as well as the ability to play through injury or not get injured at all. LeBron's twenty-two seasons dwarf Jordan's fifteen as explored in the first section of this book. Though their numbers here are both confined to what happened before and during their age 39-40 seasons, Jordan's missed time from ages eighteen to twenty-one as well as his interstitial hiatuses subtract from his overall longevity. For those who would boast Jordan's college success as part of his basketball resumé, even the Jumpman himself agrees that it was not until the midst of his collegiate career that he became a player ready for the highest level of basketball. "That turned my name from Mike to Michael Jordan," he says during the first episode of the Netflix series "The Last Dance" with reference to a game-winning shot hit at the end of his freshman season with North Carolina. "It gave me the confidence that I needed to start to excel at the game of basketball."

Both Michael Jordan and LeBron James have one season that stands out as significantly impacted by injury (Michael in 1985-86 and LeBron in 2018-19). Other than these, the two were usually on the court as long as they were on a roster. Some critics of LeBron might attempt to point out that Jordan played a higher percentage of regular season games throughout his fifteen years than LeBron did over his twenty-two. But this game-to-game availability falls entirely apart for Jordan when we realize that he took entire seasons off multiple times between the different portions of his career. LeBron happening to miss a game here or there in January or February is nothing compared to the Bulls star deciding to rest for a year and a half between 1993-1995 and again for the better part of three years from 1998-2001.

The second aspect of longevity we ought to be concerned with is the level of play throughout all eras of one's career. If the last section on *peak* was an inquiry into the highest high each of these players reached, its counterpoint will be found here in an examination of each man's career lows.

For starters, it needs to be reiterated that Michael Jordan and LeBron James did not start playing in the NBA at the same age. LeBron, coming right out of high school, began his professional career instantly while Michael played three seasons in the NCAA. This fact damages Jordan's longevity case right off the bat. It is difficult for us to compare this front end of each man's career when one of them was not even playing in the league that would qualify him for the discussion. So when it comes to the early section of their careers, we can do little else than award the *younger years* point to LeBron.

The later portion of their careers contains some of the same circumstance. Because they both reached the age of forty while playing in the NBA, we can do at least something of an apples to apples comparison though it will be somewhat tarnished by yet another multi-year absence from Michael Jordan. The best we can do is to line up their final two seasons spanning ages thirty-eight to forty and see how the two men stack up against each other. Some may wish for a larger sample size, but in order to attain such numbers, we would have to reach all the way back from 2003 into 1998 to find a season where Jordan played, and then we would be left with the quandary of how to assess another span of years where one man played and the other did not as well as what the effect of elongated rest was for one of them and how to reasonably weigh it.

Michael Jordan's final two years were played during 2001-03 with the Washington Wizards. He averaged 21.5 points, 4.5 assists, 5.9 rebounds, 1.5 steals, and 0.5 blocks. His scoring was done while taking 20.4 field goal attempts per game and shooting 43.1% from the floor.

LeBron James may indeed decide to play past his fortieth year, so we cannot definitively say these are the stats for the end of his career, but to match them with Jordan's closing age, this is what we find. In 2023-24 and 2024-25, LeBron averaged 25.1 points, 8.3 assists, 7.6 rebounds, 1.2 steals, and 0.6 blocks. His average shot attempts per game was at 18.0, and on those attempts he shot 52.7%.

The only thing Michael Jordan can boast in the later years is that he had more steals per game than his competition. There is little debate to be had. In fact, the story is less about who comes out on top and more about the drastic delta there is between the two. Throughout their prime years, it was always Jordan's claim to fame that he was the best scorer around. Indeed, he holds the record for highest career point average to this day. We have already addressed in several sections the primary reason for this being his large shooting volume compared to LeBron, and indeed that is still the case here, but for one of the few times in this discussion, we see LeBron's average points per game outdo Michael's straight on. This difference is compounded when one looks down toward the numbers on shooting efficiency. Not only did LeBron score more, but he did it with fewer shots. Nothing tells the story more than their comparative field goal percentages, a category where LeBron eclipses Jordan by nearly double digits.

In addition to the higher and more efficient scoring, the difference in rebounds is decisive and the average number of assists for LeBron approaches a doubling of his rival. Though LeBron has let out murmurings of retirement in the near future, if numbers were all we had to look at, we would all assume we were witnessing one of the game's greats in the midst of his prime.

COMPARING ERAS

19.
General Advancement

The real sticking point of basketball's GOAT debate tends to be in the fact that these two players never faced each other head to head. Of course, there is an infamous story floating around of a sixteen-year-old LeBron James joining a pick-up game with several NBA veterans, Michael Jordan being one, at a Jordan-owned establishment. But even though the young LeBron comes out looking spectacularly impressive from such accounts, it is unfair for us to use a collection of word of mouth stories as evidence, especially considering the small sample size of the event. The best we can do when it comes to comparing one era of NBA basketball to another is to elucidate the environments and changes the league went through to get an idea of how to weigh the difficulty and style of one against the other.

The first thing to acknowledge when one considers the temporal progression of a sport, and perhaps any enterprise at all, is that there will almost undoubtedly be advancement in one or all of its aspects. The players who come later on in time have a distinct advantage over their precursors because they have the ability to look back on strategies, techniques, triumphs, and pitfalls of those who came before them and use those observations to learn in a quick, secondhand fashion without the burden of discovering such things for themselves through trial. This is the case with every sport. The chess legend Garry Kasparov discusses this phenomenon at length in a 2019 conversation with Lex Fridman after being asked how he thinks about the GOAT debate in his own sport. "Any new generation knows much more about the game than the previous one. So, when people say 'Oh, Garry was the greatest, Fischer was the greatest, Magnus was the greatest,' it disregards the fact that the great players of the past...they knew so little about chess by today's standards, and today just any kid you know that's spent a few years with his or her chess computer knows much more about the game." Kasparov is right on the money with this message, and its application to basketball can be seen in a myriad of ways; most notably the rise in skill among the average player.

Back when Michael Jordan played his NBA basketball, the positional definition of each player came along with a relatively solid role and game plan. The point guard took the ball up the floor and got the offense moving, the shooting guards moved off screens and looked for shots at the basket, the power forwards and centers generally stayed close to the rim and used their big bodies in the post-up game. Nowadays, because the level of talent has risen so significantly, the five players that find themselves out on the court at any given time are generally expected to be able to do most or all of these things at a professional level. There are increasingly fewer centers in today's game that do not have a competent three point shot because it has been discovered that a big man who is a threat to shoot opens the floor up to so much more potential offense. Big men as skilled as Nikola Jokic and Victor Wembanyama are obviously the peak of this notion, but their style of play is becoming more and more the norm for players all around. Conversely, the floor becoming more open means that a smaller player with the skills to score inside becomes significantly attractive due to the fact that there will consequently be more space and opportunity for them in the post positions when they get a favorable match up.

This versatility is also a necessity on the defensive

end where constant motion and space require everyone to guard further from the basket and fluidly switch onto different types of defensive assignments throughout the play.

Our rise in skill comes first from the natural advancement of the game but it comes also from the dramatically increased pool of participants. Back in 1994, in the midst of Jordan's career, the NBA had a total of just twenty-four international players amongst its ranks. As the popularity of the game has grown throughout the decades so has the influence from other regions of the world, injecting both new skills and strategies into the game as well as more players. Today, the NBA has crossed the mark of one-hundred and twenty-five international players. And as with anything else, broadening the pool from which talent can be picked will tend to raise the overall level of competence. The increase in foreign representation in the NBA is a consequence of pure meritocracy where the best players are given the chance to compete in the league no matter where they originate. This is clearly seen through the percentage of today's stars who come from outside of the United States' borders. Nikola Jokic, Giannis Antetokounmpo, Luka Doncic, Joel Embiid, and Shai Gilgeous-Alexander are just the tip of the spear for notable foreign names dominating the modern NBA. Were the popularity and accessibility of the sport as prominent in Jordan's day as it is now, the NBA of the 1990's would have been markedly more talented.

In addition to the fact that the game has been opened up both strategically and geographically throughout the years, the eminence of today's game is helped by social and scientific factors such as advancements in health and physical fitness which allow the most talented players to both reach their fullest potential as well as stay in that prime condition for longer. Detractors may attempt to argue that if Michael Jordan had been the recipient of these luxuries that it would have enhanced his greatness too and therefore it is not a relevant point. The problem with this idea is that in order to grant Jordan the benefits of modern strategy and science we must also grant it to each one of his opponents. This rising tide tends to lift each individual ship which is a problem specifically for Jordan who relied largely on a midrange jumper and the Phil Jackson offense for his scoring, both of which we have seen wane in effectiveness since our movement into the modern era.

The retort one can expect from a Jordan apologist is that the era discussion comes down most saliently to toughness and physicality. It is certainly true that the 1980's and 1990's NBA was a more physical league with more defenders near the paint attempting to block one's way to the basket. The usual assertion is that Michael Jordan would have adapted to the increased skill of today better than LeBron James would have adapted to the physicality of the previous era. All of the evidence, however, points in a different direction. Michael's ability to adapt to the newer style of basketball will forever be a mystery in absolute terms, but the numbers that do exist can shed some light on its probability.

Michael Jordan's career three-point percentage stands at 32.7%. It ought to be noted that specifically when comparing eras a stat like three-point percentage will mean slightly different things. Because vastly more attempts are taken in the modern game and the precision of the average shooter is significantly higher, defenders are now more diligent about defending the arc. This means that despite the fact that the three-point shots are the same distance now as they were when Jordan was playing (with some notable exception), they are decidedly more difficult. Keeping this fact in mind, we can compare Jordan's success to LeBron's in career three-point accuracy at 34.9%. Even if you grant the idea that Jordan would have been a better thee point shooter than he was back in the 80's and 90's if he grew up today, you would still have to contend with the fact that the shots are more difficult now due to a defense more honed in on stopping them. These two factors seem most likely to balance out, leaving us therefore with LeBron James still on top as a distance shooter and overall more versatile and therefore more fit for the modern game.

We can assess the inverse of this idea by placing LeBron back in a more physical era where interior buckets come with a higher price. The idea that LeBron James would struggle mightily with an increase to the game's physicality is erroneous on its face. There are few single athletes in world history more physically gifted than him. The combination of size, speed, and strength possessed by the Kid from Akron is nearly unparalleled in modern sports. We can grant that any increase in physicality would likely make it more difficult for him to score on offense, but the fact that he already outdoes Jordan in 2 point field goal percentage by a considerable margin (55.5% to 51.0%) leads one to believe that at worst the two would draw near a tie in this category. Then the flip side of the physicality argument must also be taken into account. If an increased amount of brute force from defenders would make things harder on LeBron James going to the hole, then we must also grant him an equal amount of increased defensive production since the athletic juggernaut would himself be allowed to use his physical gifts to stop offensive players he was guarding. In the end, these three aspects of the game (interior play, perimeter play, and defense) end up favoring LeBron James in at least two out of three categories no matter which era you try to place him in.

A quick aside needs to be made about the three-point line itself. A notable exception to the distance of the arc was alluded to above in reference to the 1994 decision by the league to shorten its length from the basket. A concerted effort was put forth through rule changes to increase the amount of scoring seen in the league. One such change was in moving the three-point line in from its original spot at 23'9" to 22". The shortened line existed in the league until 1997, so while its presence was not the norm for Jordan's entire career, he did benefit from it in such numbers as his career three-point percentage and even won one of his championship titles during this time.

20.
Expansion Era

There are other curious facts that often get lost in the comparison between eras, and that is because they didn't happen on the court, yet their influence on what happened there was enormous.

As the popularity of basketball continues to grow, the pools of players and fans have historically demanded an increasingly larger league as the home of the sport. This results in periodic additions to the NBA, many of which have happened in the last few decades. But there was a particular period of years, namely from 1988 to 1995, where professional basketball in America saw a seismic boom. In just those seven short years, the league decided to add six new franchises. Such development requires, most obviously, players to fill the roster on the new franchise. But where do the new players come from? Since it would be an incredible disadvantage to the new team to have no one on their squad who was previously good enough to play in the NBA, the way they get their players is primarily by selecting them from existing teams. If there are multiple new franchises entering the league, then there is a special expansion draft aside from the regular NBA draft where the newcomers take turns picking their players from current pros. Of course, not all players are up for grabs. Those franchises already present are allowed to protect a portion of their roster, thus saving them from losing a star player through no fault of their own. But the younger talent often goes unprotected which has palpable downstream effects.

This process is ultimately a great thing for the health of the NBA and basketball in general as it allows new talent and influence into the league as well as spreads the popularity of the sport to new geographical markets. However, during the process, it can complicate the current basketball landscape a bit. Because cemented professionals are being taken from the teams that purposely drafted or traded for them, it can mess with that team's vision of their roster construction and therefore dilute the pool of potentially talented, cohesive teams. This effect is immediate and often ripples forward a few years until those players can be properly replaced. Were this to happen just once over a decade or two it would probably go virtually unnoticed. But a repeated barrage of stolen players can cause tremendous upheaval to the growth of organizations, and this is precisely what occurred during and immediately preceding the years that Michael Jordan did all of his winning.

In 1988 it was the Charlotte Hornets and the Miami Heat who entered the league. The following season saw the additions of both the Minnesota Timberwolves and the Orlando Magic. Then in 1995 the NBA's gates opened toward Canada to welcome the Vancouver Grizzlies and the Toronto Raptors to the club. In total, seventy-three professional players were forcibly moved from their originally contracted team to one of these expansion squads. One might argue this is meaningless since each of the existing teams were picked from an equal number of times. But in truth, expansion drafts are more detrimental to teams that are in the process of building whereas teams with a stable core of protected stars will be more resilient to the waves of lost players. One such team was the Chicago Bulls. Since they had already established a well-rounded set of consistent players, the loss of others didn't have as strong a sting. But other teams who were less solidly built those particular seasons were left even further diluted. This phenomenon cannot be used to entirely explain the Bulls' dominance of the 1990's but they were certainly helped by its consistent scrambling of their potential opponents.

The assertion that such changes attenuated the league's talent is not one that is confined to this book. The now coach of the Los Angeles Lakers and long time NBA pro, JJ Redick, came under a bit of a spotlight in 2024 when discussing these facts. "Jordan was drafted during his heyday, and six teams were added to the NBA," said Redick. "There were ninety players added to the NBA...Does that not water down the regular season to a degree?" These comments reignited the discussion of the 1990's weaker distribution of talent in the modern age, but for those who would claim that this is a new conversation, there is ample evidence of big-time voices from Jordan's own era, and even his own team, saying the exact same things.

"I just think the league has really filtered out and diluted itself. I just think it's kind of hurting the league right now." These words came from the mouth of Dennis Rodman, one of the largest pieces in Jordan's career success.

The great Larry Bird echoed the sentiment too by saying, "Well, I think the expansion teams really hurt the league. I think it's depleted some of the talent of our league."

Furthermore, if the iconic players of the time weren't enough to convince one that attenuation was part of the league's fabric in the 1990's, we might look to the coaches and NBA media for further evidence. Jerry Sloan, the coach of the Utah Jazz in 1996, said "You look at the overall picture; it is diluted to some extent. You can get by with three great players on a team and have a chance to win it all. Before, you had to have four or five great players, and some good players around them."

Not only was Sloan's comment made in the midst of the problematic years, but it was reported on in articles such as Richard Evans' 1996 publication "NBA Rosters Diluted Thanks To Expansion," wherein the writer makes the argues that while there are some good teams in the 1996

NBA, there are no great ones. Publications such as this go to show the real sentiments on the league back then, facts that are threatened with dissolution from those who want to pretend differently simply to benefit the reputations of previous players.

21.
Rule Changes

Aside from the strange roster changes that occurred league-wide during Jordan's reign, there are some other off-the-court differences between the times our two GOATs played which should be addressed. These come primarily in the form of rule changes. While basketball has maintained its general look and set of rules throughout the decades, there are significant changes in style of play that in some cases are not simply due to the advancement of strategy and skill.

For instance, in 2004, the NBA officially parted ways with *hand checking*. This refers to a defensive player using his hands on a dribbling offensive player in order to stop him from getting an angle toward the basket. Taking the hand check away resulted in a boost of scoring from 93 points per game to 97 the year after the change. Many Jordan fans will insist this difference is evidence that LeBron could not have scored at the high rate he did if he'd played in Jordan's era because the defense was more stringent. But this is laughable. While allowing a hand check necessarily makes a defense at least marginally tougher, the combination of size, strength, and speed that LeBron possesses is far too potent to be deterred by the presence of a hand. The number of times we have seen LeBron nonchalantly finish through contact should be evidence enough for this. Hand checking, remember, did not allow defenders to grab, pull, or push with the arms to any significant degree, nor was it allowed in the scoring area near the rim.

Anyone claiming LeBron would not be able to succeed in a more physical era is appealing to an unfalsifiable narrative of their imagination, and it needs to be noted that LeBron is not uniquely accused benefitting from easier defense. Michael Jordan in his own right was stuck with the label as the chief beneficiary of a softer game by some of his peers. Isiah Thomas even years later spoke of the different whistle Jordan received in his era: "Y'all want [Jordan] to win. Y'all change all the rules so he can win. These are the facts. I go down the lane, I get my ass beat. You see pictures of Michael Cooper scratching Larry Bird's jersey off, right? You see Kevin Mchale slamming Kurt Rambis to the Floor...Everybody getting hit. Oh, but [Jordan] can't get hit? So we going to change all the rules so he can dunk. Because they marketing the dunk." So if Michael Jordan himself was once upon a time receiving the same type of criticism his proponents now use to argue for his superiority, we can and should recognize this as either a point without a strong basis that will fade into the ether or hold its weight equally against both Jordan and LeBron.

On the flip side of that coin of defensive toughness, if one were to argue that the absence of hand checking made defenses that guarded LeBron easier to penetrate, then they would also be forced to acknowledge that the defensive rules Jordan played under favored him on that end of the floor. Any attempt to subtract from LeBron's offensive production through the loss or presence of hand checking must be equally applied to Jordan's defensive production since it was an advantage he was allowed to use.

But for as much air time as the hand checking rule gets in such debates, there is another rule change that occurred in 2001 with just as much impact. When we look back at Jordan's era we often see a collection of three or four defenders huddled on one side of the court even if the ball happened to be opposite them. This amount of space is puzzling for anyone playing today's game where help defense is essential to guard against drives when another defender gets beat or closes out too hard on a shooter.

The immense amount of space we see in certain pre-2000's situations was a result of an abandoned rule called *illegal defense*. The concept of illegal defense was that a defensive player was not allowed to play in a zone coverage or anything resembling a zone. This meant a defender must either fully commit to a double team or fully commit to his individual man. There was no hedging between players allowed, no flooding the box from the weak side allowed, no fake double teams to force a pass allowed; nothing but sticking to your man or committing to a double. This stringent style made for imbalances on the court that are just not seen in today's game; and for good reason as they allow easier shot creating situations such as isolations in the post and half a court of open space around the ball.

The NBA realized this was bad for the game, and when 2001 came around they abolished the illegal defense rule and replaced it with a more tepid version: *defensive three seconds*. This new rule allowed defenders to roam wherever they please and help their teammates so long as they did not spend a full three seconds in the paint without actively guarding their man or the ball.

Now that the rules have been changed to allow more defensive freedom, we see substantially more sophisticated defensive schemes than we ever did in the 1990's. The constant rotation and help defense of today's NBA requires players to not only have the physical abilities to cover more of the court but the mental acumen to anticipate what the offense will do so that they can make it to their new, shifting assignment in time. Such advanced defensive play is desperately needed since the skill of the offensive players has risen so dramatically. The days of simple man-to-man basketball are over unless a team is willing to give up wide open looks every time down the floor.

22.
Idol Worship

In 1995, Michael Jordan received enough votes to place him eleventh in the MVP race. This sounds like a down year for the Bulls' star until one realizes that Jordan participated in only seventeen games that season. Today, there are stipulations that would preclude votes cast for a player who was absent for 80% of the season, but even before those rules were set in place, the fact that Jordan's reputation was enough to garner him such recognition is evidence that we on the side of LeBron James have a problem. It is undoubtedly the most intractable part of Jordan's case as the greatest of all time. This problem is a tricky one to deal with because it does not reside in the record books, nor can it be caught on film. Its place of rest is instead within the hearts and minds of the acolytes who praise His Airness. We're talking, of course, about the charismatic awe that Michael Jordan injected into the NBA when he rose to the peak of his powers. The stories from onlookers are filled with an inspired sort of reverence when they talk about how they had never seen anything like this Michael Jordan before. He played with a dominant will to win and angelic athleticism that let him glide through the air in a manner not so much human as it was heavenly. And, in part, they are right.

After an entire book's worth of comparisons, it may be tempting to fall into a disrespectful attitude toward the Chicago legend. But this would be a mistake. Too much of the world of sports discussion is taken up by exaggerators and polemicists focusing on the minute flaws in the skills or personalities of our stars which leads to disingenuous lines of argument and sometimes altogether incorrect assumptions. We have seen how this effect has cast its shadow on the legacy of LeBron James with things like the decision to go to Miami, the misguided perception of his folding late in games, and the conviction that his records are feats of simple lifetime achievement rather than due to a height of excellence. We know these things are straw men, and it would be just as ridiculous to turn the tables and attempt to slander Michael Jordan. He is, after all, one of the greatest athletes in recorded history. This sober mindset must take on a wider lens to help explain what is the particular flavor of undying adoration for Michael Jordan.

The first aspect of Jordan's idolization has already been partly described. It is in those contemporary onlookers' astonishment at his athleticism and style of play. Whenever ground is broken, in any field be it sport, business, or technology, the immediate, reactive excitement sears itself into a person's mind. It is a fact of our human psychology that we are specially attuned to recognizing patterns and, consequently, those things that break the mould to forge a new viable path by which to journey. Michael Jordan was one of these mould breakers, a trailblazer whose style could not be ignored. His play was effective, but more than that, it was gorgeous. On court actions combined with his intangible, and sometimes ineffable, qualities of charisma, willpower, and iconic idiosyncrasies to create an aura around the man that was bigger than basketball. The evidence for this unique stardom is everywhere. From cereal boxes to the Hollywood screen and countless commercials, Michael Jordan's face was and remains ubiquitous in our culture. The Jumpman logo is probably more popular and symbolic of the game of basketball than the NBA's own, modeled after the great Jerry West in 1969. One need not step onto a court or even be in the company of ball players in order to look down and see one of the dozens of Jordan brand shoes that subsume much of American style. The Jordan brand has only continued to grow as the years go on, bringing in a whopping seven billion dollars in revenue in 2024 alone. And that number, rivaling the population of the entire planet, illustrates how in some ways we are not dealing with a man confined to the somewhat narrow realm of sports.

We would not go as far as to say that Michael Jordan was the first basketball player to reach past sports and into general celebrity, but he was certainly the one who succeeded in carrying it the furthest.

It was not, however, simply on television and in the streets and sneaker stores where Jordan was revered as an entity larger than life. This idolization was cast in solid bronze on November 1, 1994 when a statue of the Chicago legend was unveiled. Standing twelve feet tall and weighing two-thousand pounds, the sculpture depicts Jordan in his famous "Jumpman" pose. The salience of this statue, though, is in its inscription. Etched into the black granite base are the words, "The best there ever was. The best there ever will be." It is not a record book; it is not a vote; it is only a statue made to immortalize the franchise's most beloved player. But the spirit contained in those carved words is quite troubling for those looking to have an honest discussion about who the greatest player ever is or who is even eligible for the conversation. There is no doubt that some people can look past those words and have an opinion in one era that they change in the years to come, but there is also no doubt that some people find themselves locked into a position. This sentiment was captured wonderfully through the words of Kenny "The Jet" Smith during an NBA roundtable when the topic of someone displacing Jordan as the greatest ever arose. "...you're not Jordan," says Smith, "because you can't break a ground that hadn't been broken yet. I don't see that LeBron is going to break a ground...so, he will never be that. He will be a great player, but he'll never be a groundbreaker."

What we're seeing here from Kenny Smith, who was in his own right a great player, is an opinion carried by many that pervades the GOAT debate but really has little if anything to do with basketball. The argument being made here is a psychological one; it is the contention that being the first to do something holds a weight to it that over-powers other categories of accomplishment. There are many faults in this line of thinking, but we shall address the most glaring one by asking the question: what ground did Michael Jordan break? The answer is in the first of the two sentences inscribed on the Jumpman statue. The ground Jordan broke was in becoming the greatest to ever play basketball. This should strike discord in one's brain since it only stands to reason that before Michael Jordan was the best of all time, someone else must have been the best of all time. So what does it mean for someone to make that type of Kenny Smith argument? What is meant through that sentiment is that Jordan was the first person *they*, that particular viewer, saw become the greatest of all time. They are making an argument that goes along the lines of, *No one else could ever produce in me the feelings of awe and appreciation that I had for Jordan.* And in that, they are likely correct. It is often the fact that we hold a special, perhaps even irrational, place in our hearts and minds for the first great album we ever heard, the first great vacation we went on, the first love we ever fell into, and the first time we saw a man defy the odds of sport. But those feelings do not hold sway in a real discussion of greatness. They are personal, and they are important, but they have little bearing on the reality we all must share.

One can see how much the argument of *breaking ground* ties cognitive knots in the minds of those who subscribe to it by simply watching further on in the same broadcast where Kenny Smith walks back his own rationale when discussing other players. "...as great as Shaq was... everyone always says, 'Well, Wilt.' Now Shaq, greatest player we've ever seen at his position...but he's always, because Wilt was the groundbreaker, so he never gets that, all the credit he probably deserves he can't break through that Wilt comparison." Smith offers his praise for Shaquille O'Neil and believes that the big man deserves more credit than he historically gets when being overshadowed by a *groundbreaker* comparison. What we're seeing here, and what we see all too often, is a line of argument that originates from a viewer's anecdotal experiences the game. This leads us psychologically into that second sentence of the inscription on Jordan's statue: "The best there ever will be." Obviously, this is a statement of faith and fandom, but for some who employ arguments like those just seen above, it is a statement taken as inescapable fact. And people who believe such things will search out facts in order to reverse engineer evidence for their convictions. For the men and women in the Church of Jordan, the reverse engineered evidence is in things like Michael's 6-0 NBA Finals record.

Zero, dear reader, is a very special number, and it is often the core of nonsensical argumentation. As we discussed in previous sections, the fact that Jordan never lost in the Finals does not mean he never lost, but for those looking to spin statistics into a story, it provides the basis to pretend that he never lost. One need only convince himself that a personal Finals record is the only thing that matters, or is at least a preeminent factor, and then it is clear to see that since zero is the least number of losses a person can have, it de facto points to the idea that no one is mathematically able to beat Jordan. One could, in that erroneous theory, tie him, but no one could ever do better.

There also remains a litany of factors contributing to Jordan's mythos that find their roots in the media landscape both back in his era and today. The most prevalent difference between eras of media is the rise of the internet and the twenty-four hour news cycle. The effect this has had on athletic discourse has been huge for several reasons. First and foremost is the simple fact of a dramatically increased level of scrutiny on today's players. As the

2024-25 season has evolved, we have waded into a widespread discussion of the NBA media's relationship with today's players, one that is far more negative than it could be. When Anthony Edwards was asked what he thought about potentially becoming the new face of the league once legends like LeBron, Steph Curry, and Kevin Durant are out of the picture, Edwards responded with a bit of derision toward the idea. "No. Not really...That's what they got Wemby for," said Edwards. He went on to elaborate, "I'm capable of being that guy, but I don't want to be that guy. Put it like that. I want to be the guy to just show up and hoop and just kill dudes and go home." These comments inspired disdain in some commentators who feel star players should not eschew such roles as ambassadors of the game. But the King himself came to Edwards defense shortly after.

When asked about the situation LeBron said, "Why do you want to be the face of the league when all the people that cover our game and talk about our game on a day-to-day basis s— on everybody?" This in turn sparked more controversy as it challenged the NBA media to reflect on the negative way the league is often covered.

This exchange between LeBron, Anthony Edwards, and the media is only one instance, but it is illustrative of the boiling point that was finally reached after years of constant scrutiny, a type of attention that is new to sports in an era where games are aired on many different networks, each who have their own crew, most of whom grew up playing or watching a previous era's style of basketball and may understandably be nostalgically connected to it. And it is not only the television networks airing the games who have voice nowadays. The rise of the internet has cultivated a landscape of thousands of voices with substantially wider reach than any regular citizen could have hoped for thirty years ago. And much like cultural or political news, when the world of sports commentators have to vie against such enormous odds they will often resort to negatively framed arguments or name calling in attempt to pique audience attention. It's no surprise to those of the internet age that negativity tends to drive much of the consumption of news media no matter the field. The old sentiment of *if it bleeds, it leads* therefore became co-opted in the sports world to something more like *if it's mean, it's seen.* Such disrespectful commentary came to the forefront of the league's attention when Stephen A. Smith, the highly paid and long tenured ESPN pundit, made insulting and unfounded remarks toward LeBron James' parenting in regards to the latter's son playing in the NBA. Such comments have nothing to do with LeBron's basketball play, yet the observation that they continued to make headlines in the news is a perfect illustration of the negative light under which many of today's stars find themselves being covered, LeBron James chief among them.

These facts shed light on some of the earlier conundrums discovered in this book. Take, for instance, the backwards relationship between LeBron James and Michael Jordan's clutch shooting numbers compared with their reputations. Despite the fact that LeBron's success in big moments outdoes Jordan's both in cumulative totals and percentages, he has had to fight a reputation of a poor clutch performer while Jordan continues to ride on nearly godlike status in that department. This discrepancy is likely due to the fact that virtually every professional game LeBron James ever played was watched, recorded, and scrutinized by thousands the night of and day after. Any small mistake he made was able to be isolated and discussed in painstaking detail on hour-long talk shows dedicated only to sports; the likes of Skip Bayless often flowing over into long monologues of speculative criticism toward the King. And while such discussion actually does nothing to affect the basketball that was played by either Jordan or LeBron, it does do a substantial amount in shaping the understanding of the game for more casual or younger fans who do not have the basketball acumen or historical knowledge to develop sophisticated opinions of their own.

Now, were Jordan to have emerged in a media landscape that was similar to that of the 2000's, 2010's, and 2020's, there would be no reason to point all of this out. However, the 1980's and 90's were a very different place. The news was far less prevalent, and that which did discuss the athletes was far more succinct. Networks and content creators did not have to stoop to negativity to drive ratings. If they did, one could imagine a number of daily exposés on Jordan's smoking and gambling habits, a whirlwind of negativity that could drive some into disliking the star and casting aspersions on him in all domains. These too would have been unfair to use in a way that has any effect on his basketball legacy; luckily for His Airness, he did not have to endure the all-prying eyes and mouths of today's media. No, for Michael Jordan, the media was different. It was largely a supportive arm of Michael's legacy, and even when it wasn't, there was the safety of certain media relationships to take refuge in.

In the 1993 playoffs, Michael Jordan began to ignore the media. His personal boycott was in response to some scrutiny he was receiving based on reports of his gambling debts. When he finally decided to address the topic, he did it intentionally and to the sole ears of NBC's Ahmad Rashad. Rashad, a former NFL receiver turned sports broadcaster, had become friends with Michael Jordan and through this relationship gained exclusive access to all things Chicago Bulls. After "The Last Dance," a docuseries on Jordan and the Bulls was released, Rashad used the following words to reflect on his time covering the squad. "My job as a sideline reporter was to get insights and interview the star of the game after the game, who just happened to be Michael, who just happened to be one of my best friends."

This situation presents a stark contrast to the way the media relates to LeBron James. While there certainly are prominent voices on both television and the internet who have supported LeBron throughout the years and have given him honest credit when it was due, there are no reporters who self describe as one of his best friends simultaneously being a key valve for information on him and his team. Magic Johnson too reminisces on how the night before he called Game 1 of the Bulls' Finals against the Portland Trailblazers he had spent the evening playing cards with Michael Jordan in the comfort of his very own home.

In light of all of this, we can track down the ethereal portion of Jordan's legend. The basketball was incredible, but the cultural impact was just as great, and it is the cultural impact which is not allowed a seat at the table of honest debate. Similarly, such fallacious points of contention like the importance of zero losses in the Finals, must be dispensed with. They are little more than semantic tricks, whether consciously or unconsciously employed. And the effects of these tricks are poisonous as their main consequence is to reinforce the presumption etched into the last sentence of Jordan's statue; "The best there ever will be." Those Jordan fans who deploy such arguments have trapped themselves into an everlasting opinion. The very letters of that inscription are like steel bars binding the mind of the apologist in a prison cell whose key is nothing more than honest inquiry. This image of a self-imposed mental prison is one of our great saving graces as people who champion the GOAT case of LeBron James; for while we call him the best now, it does not mean we declare him the prohibitive greatest going forward. There will undoubtedly be some who step up the dais to challenge the throne. Just in the last few years we have seen the game evolve with the shooting of Steph Curry, the athleticism and frame of Giannis Antetokounmpo, and the alien combination of skill and height of Victor Wembanyama. It would not be impossible for such a talent to come through and claim a new GOAT status. We can watch it, and the fact that we can even enjoy it is the needle on a compass of reason that tells us, as LeBron fans, we are free.

23.
Recap

The preceding pages contain a lot of information and context to take in. With the aim of providing a digestible, truncated version of the arguments made above, we shall list most of the salient points in bite-sized form.

1. Virtually all of the cumulative numbers are in LeBron's favor (with the exception of steals which are fraught with fraudulence).
2. While Jordan scored more on a per-game basis, LeBron scored far more efficiently, and when shooting percentages and total shot attempts are taken into account it is plain to see that LeBron was a better overall scorer.
3. LeBron's career showcases more sustained success while Jordan took several breaks.
4. LeBron has significantly more versatility on both offense and defense which requires more skill and preparation.
5. Jordan played in an era of more compacted and imbalanced spacing.
6. Their DPOY awards (Jordan 1, LeBron 0) should very arguably be flipped due to the documented errors in Jordan's numbers and the 2013 controversy with Marc Gasol.
7. LeBron had better clutch numbers both in a game's last moments and in elimination games.
8. LeBron has won championships with three separate

organizations, proving he can adapt to new circumstances whereas Jordan did all of his winning with a similar Bulls roster.

9. Jordan is hardly even a winning player when not playing under Phil Jackson. LeBron, on the other hand, has won with three different coaches, none of whom have won a ring without him nor have any of LeBron's seven other coaches ever won an NBA title.

10. Jordan only ever won one single playoff game without Scottie Pippen by his side. LeBron has won continually in the playoffs despite having several notably bad supporting casts.

11. Jordan got to shoot from the NBA's shorter three-point line (1994-1997).

12. Though LeBron played with several talented teammates, the talent on Jordan's Bulls was more conducive to creating a cohesive roster.

13. In 1994-95, the Bulls won only two fewer games without Jordan while any team LeBron has left has imploded.

14. In the Finals, LeBron played against better players.

15. In the Finals, LeBron played against four times as many DPOY candidates (top 5) as Jordan did.

16. When Jordan played against great players in the Finals they were virtually always lone stars on their team whereas LeBron routinely had to face dynastic teams with several All-Stars combined.

17. LeBron has the better single game, winning streak/partial season, whole season, and stretch of three seasons. In order to give the *peak* argument to Michael, one would have to define it quite narrowly.

18. LeBron's longevity has Jordan beaten at both the beginning and the end of their careers.

19. The level of competition has simply gotten much better over the years due to a larger global pool and general advancement of skills and strategy.

20. Due to the advancement in the basketball world's skill and strategy, the defense that had to be played in LeBron's era was significantly more complex.
21. Jordan played in a watered down expansion era.
22. The pace of play during Jordan's career was faster which gave him several more possessions per game to rack up stats.
23. Jordan proponents are often logically locked into positions by the way their arguments are formulated, therefore creating dishonest, or at least unfair, parameters for discussion.

Bibliography

Acedera, Shane Garry. "Mike Dunleavy Says James Worthy's Injury Hurt the Lakers ..." Mike Dunleavy Says James Worthy's Injury Hurt the Lakers' Chances in the 1991 NBA Finals: "We Really Felt Good about Our Chances There," Basketball Network, 1 Jan. 2025, www.basket ballnetwork.net/latest-news/mike-dunleavy-says-wor thys-injury-hurt-the-lakers-chances-in-the-1991-finals.

Admin. "Michael Jordan Statue at the United Center: Chica go Bulls." The Official Site of the NBA for the Latest NBA Scores, Stats & News., NBA, 13 Jan. 2011, www. nba.com/bulls/history/jordanstatuehtml.

Aldridge, David. "Lakers Are Injured, Hurting for Solu tions against Bulls - The Washington Post." Washing ton Post, 11 June 1991, www.washingtonpost.com/ archive/sports/1991/06/12/lakers-are-injured-hurting-for-solutions-against-bulls/c3b219c5-0110-4333-ad53-20e130dfb1be/.

"All Time Leaders: Stats." NBA, www.nba.com/stats/all time-leaders. Accessed 2 Apr. 2025.

Badenhausen, Kurt. "Nike Revenue Disappoints, but Jordan Brand Hits $7B FOR YEAR." Sportico.Com, Spor tico.com, 27 June 2024, www.sportico. com/business/commerce/2024/nike-revenue-jor dan-brand-billion-1234785967/.

Baer, Jack. "NBA Playoffs 2025: Timberwolves Eliminate Lak ers Behind 20-20 Game From Rudy Gobert." Yahoo! Sports, Yahoo!, 1 May 2025, sports.yahoo.com/nba/ article/nba-playoffs-2025-timberwolves-elimi nate-lakers-behind-20-20-game-from-rudy-gob ert-045453926.html

Bhussey. "Summary of Expansion Draft Rules: Charlotte Hor nets." Official Site of the NBA for the Latest NBA Scores, Stats & News., NBA, 14 Apr. 2004, www.nba. com/hornets/news/draft_central_expansion_rules_sum mary.html.

Conway, Tyler. "Lakers' Marc Gasol on LeBron James-DPOY: 'We Can Talk over It with Some Wine.'" Bleacher Re port, Bleacher Report, 6 Dec. 2020, syndication. bleacherreport.com/amp/2921126-lakers-marc-gasol-on-LeBron-james- dpoy-we-can-talk-over-it-with-some-wine.amp.html

Clutch Time. "Isiah Thomas On NBA Changing The Rules For Jordan To Win." YouTube, YouTube, 16 Aug. 2023, https://youtube.com/shorts/oCgqqsicwmU?si=UIBuy DOJsuA4OCkL

De Lune, Claire. "LeBron James Is Doing Something He's Never Done Before: Everything." SBNa tion, SBNation, 30, Apr. 2025, https://www.sbnation. com/nba/2025/4/30/24420302/nba-playoffs-lakers-leb ron-james-role-history

Dotson, Kevin. "How Lakers Guard Jerry West's Silhouette Inspired the NBA Logo." CNN, Cable News Network, 12 June 2024, amp.cnn.com/cnn/2024/06/12/sport/jer ry-west-obit-nba-logo-spt-intl.

"Episode One." *The Last Dance.* Directed by Jason Hehir, Pro
duced by ESPN Films and Netflix, 2020,
Netflix. https://www.netflix.com/us/title/80203144?s=i
&trkid=268410292&vlang=en

"Episode Two." *The Last Dance.* Directed by Jason Hehir,
Produced by ESPN Films and Netflix, 2020,
Netflix. https://www.netflix.com/us/title/80203144?s=i
&trkid=268410292&vlang=en

"Episode Three." *The Last Dance.* Directed by Jason Hehir,
Produced by ESPN Films and Netflix, 2020,
Netflix. https://www.netflix.com/us/title/80203144?s=i
&trkid=268410292&vlang=en

"Episode Four." *The Last Dance.* Directed by Jason Hehir,
Produced by ESPN Films and Netflix, 2020,
Netflix. https://www.netflix.com/us/title/80203144?s=i
&trkid=268410292&vlang=en

"Episode Five." *The Last Dance.* Directed by Jason Hehir,
Produced by ESPN Films and Netflix, 2020,
Netflix. https://www.netflix.com/us/title/80203144?s=i
&trkid=268410292&vlang=en

"Episode Six." *The Last Dance.* Directed by Jason Hehir,
Produced by ESPN Films and Netflix, 2020,
Netflix. https://www.netflix.com/us/title/80203144?s=i
&trkid=268410292&vlang=en

"Episode Seven." *The Last Dance.* Directed by Jason Hehir,
Produced by ESPN Films and Netflix, 2020,
Netflix. https://www.netflix.com/us/title/80203144?s=i
&trkid=268410292&vlang=en

"Episode Eight." *The Last Dance.* Directed by Jason Hehir,

Produced by ESPN Films and Netflix, 2020,
Netflix. https://www.netflix.com/us/title/80203144?s=i
&trkid=268410292&vlang=en

"Episode Nine." *The Last Dance.* Directed by Jason Hehir,
Produced by ESPN Films and Netflix, 2020,
Netflix. https://www.netflix.com/us/title/80203144?s=i
&trkid=268410292&vlang=en

"Episode Ten." *The Last Dance.* Directed by Jason Hehir,
Produced by ESPN Films and Netflix, 2020,
Netflix. https://www.netflix.com/us/title/80203144?s=i
&trkid=268410292&vlang=en

ESPN Throwback. "LeBron James' High School Team Upsets
No. 1 Oak Hill Academy (2002) | ESPN Archive."
YouTube, 22 Mar. 2020, www.youtube.com/
watch?v=2nC9z57MuaI.

Evans, Richard. "NBA Rosters Diluted Thanks to Expansion."
Deseret News, Deseret News, 22 Jan. 2024, www.
deseret.com/1996/1/5/19217469/nba-rosters-dilut
ed-thanks-to-expansion/.

Fridman, Lex. "Garry Kasparov: Chess, Deep Blue, AI, and
Putin." Spotify, 27 Oct. 2019, open.spotify.com/epi
sode/6JRpPEFhkd9qNjUAwxmYCS.

Fuente, Homero De la. "Paul Silas, 3-Time NBA Champion
Player and Coach, Dead at 79." CNN, Cable News
Network, 12 Dec. 2022, amp.cnn.com/cnn/2022/12/11/
us/paul-silas-nba-player-coach-obit-spt-intl.

Ganglani, Nicole. How Removing the Hand Check Rule
Changed the NBA Forever - Basketball Network - Your
Daily Dose of Basketball, Basketball Network, 4 Nov.
2022, www.basketballnetwork.net/old-school/

how-removing-the-hand-check-rule-changed-the-nba-forever.

Ganguli, Tania. "LeBron James' First Season with Lakers Is Over." Los Angeles Times, Los Angeles Times, 30 Mar. 2019, www.latimes.com/sports/lakers/la-sp-LeBron-james-lakers-20190330-story.html.

Haberstroh, Tom. "A Closer Look at Michael Jordan's 1988 DPOY Award Raises Questions about Its Validity. Has LeBron James Been Chasing a Ghost?" Yahoo! Sports, Yahoo!, 20 June 2024, sports.yahoo. com/a-closer-look-at-michael-jordans-1988-dpoy-award-raises-questions-about-its-validity-has-LeBron-james-been-chasing-a-ghost-140452567.html.

Kimble, Julian. "Rewind: Ahmad Rashad on 30 Years of 'NBA Inside Stuff.'" The Ringer, 27 Oct. 2020, www.thering er.com/2020/10/27/nba/nba-inside-stuff-ahmad-rashad.

Leahy, Sean. "Stephen A. Smith on Courtside Moment with LeBron James: 'That Wasn't a Basketball Player Con fronting Me. That Was a Parent, That Was a Father.'" Yahoo! Sports, Yahoo!, 7 Mar. 2025, sports.yahoo.com/ nba/article/stephen-a-smith-on-courtside-moment-with-LeBron-james-that-wasnt-a-basketball-player-confront ing-me-that-was-a-parent-that-was-a-father-165148593. html.

"LeBron James: Forward: Los Angeles Lakers." NBA, www. nba.com/stats/player/2544/shooting?Season=2003-04. Accessed 2 Apr. 2025.

"LeBron James Pbb Stats." Pbpstats_client, www.pbpstats. com/. Accessed 2 Apr. 2025.

"Looking Back: LeBron James' 10 Trips to the Finals." NBA,

www.nba.com/LeBron-james-past-finals-trips-history. Accessed 2 Apr. 2025.

Mahoney, Brian. "NBA Finals | Cavs' Hughes Toughing It Out." The Seattle Times, The Seattle Times Company, 10 June 2007, www.seattletimes.com/sports/nba-finals-cavs-hughes-toughing-it-out/.

Mathur, Ashish. "NBA Scorekeeper Who Gave Stats to Michael Jordan Even When He Didn't Earn Them Went into Bull's Locker Room and Said 'See MJ, We Take Care of You.'" Hoops Wire, 28 Apr. 2024, hoopswire.com/nba-scorekeeper-gave-stats-michael-jordan-bulls-news-rumors/.

Merrell, Chloe. "NBA: All-Time List of Longest Winning Streaks." NBA: All-Time List of Longest Winning Streaks, IOC, 6 Jan. 2025, www.olympics.com/en/news/all-time-list-nba-longest-winning-streaks.

Moore, Matt. "A Betting Odds History of the 1990s Chicago Bulls Dynasty." Action Network, The Action Network, 9 Dec. 2021, www.actionnetwork.com/nba/betting-odds-history-1990s-chicago-bulls-dynasty-michael-jordan.

NBA. "Michael Jordan's Got 10 Steals in One Game!" YouTube, YouTube, 31 Aug. 2022, https://youtu.be/x63V0I5T-zA?si=aPOSC1OGjswDZIRH

"NBA & ABA Career Leaders and Records for True Shooting Pct." Basketball Reference, www.basketball-reference.com/leaders/ts_pct_career.html. Accessed 2 Apr. 2025.

NBA League Averages - per Game, Basketball Reference, www.basketball-reference.com/leagues/NBA_stats_per_game.html. Accessed 2 Apr. 2025.

NBA Open Court. "NBA Open Court - The Frontcourt." You Tube, YouTube, 2 July 2017, www.youtube.com/watch?v=LcyG7QdY9No.

"The NBA's 75th Anniversary Team, Ranked: Where 76 Basketball Legends Check in on Our List." ESPN Internet Ventures, 31 July 2022, www.espn.com/nba/story/_/id/33297498/the-nba-75th-anniversary-team-ranked-where-76-basketball-legends-check-our-list.

Paine, Neil. "Where This Year's Cavs Rank among LeBron's NBA Finals Supporting Casts." FiveThirtyEight, FiveThirtyEight, 1 June 2015, fivethirtyeight.com/features/where-this-years-cavs-rank-among-LeBrons-nba-finals-supporting-casts/.

Pandey, Manish. "LeBron James and Stephen A. Smith: What's The Beef About?" BBC News, BBC, 27 Mar. 2025, www.bbc.com/news/articles/c5yr16n5zg8o.amp

"Phil Jackson Calls Scottie Pippen a BETTER Overall Player than Michael Jordan." Edited by TPGC High lights, YouTube, YouTube, 29 June 2021, www.youtube.com/watch?v=89yWdi54_7U.

Pippen, Scottie, et al. *Unguarded*. Simon & Schuster Audio, 2021. New York, NY.

Press, The Associated. "A Look at the Coaches Who Have Led Teams with LeBron James on the Roster." AP News, AP News, 3 May 2024, apnews.com/article/LeBron-james-nba-coaches-d625f623739fd83f72a94aaa344b7c.

Robertson, Claire E., et al. "Negativity Drives Online News Consumption." Nature News, Nature Publishing Group, 16 Mar. 2023, www.nature.com/articles/s41562-023-

01538-4.

Richardson, Shandel. "DID Expansion Create a Watered-down NBA during Michael Jordan Era?" Back In The Day Hoops On SI, Sports Illustrated, 29 June 2024, www.si.com/fannation/backinthedaynba/did-expansion-create-a-watered-down-nba-during-michael-jordan-era-01j1hwnjzg30#:~:text=Dennis%20Rodman%2C%20who%20was%20one,Larry%20Bird%20had%20to%20say.

Richardson, Shandel. "Three-Time All-Star Claims Michael Jordan Wanted To Team With Larry Bird In 1980s." Back In The Day Hoops On SI, Sports Illustrated, 20 Mar. 2025, https://www.si.com/fannation/backintheday nba/three-time-all-star-claims-michael-jordan-wanted-to-team-with-larry-bird-in-1980s-01jprq8j0ffr

Schilken, Chuck. "LeBron James Gets Why Anthony Edwards Doesn't Want to Be Face of NBA: 'There's This Weird Energy.'" Los Angeles Times, Los Angeles Times, 28 Feb. 2025, www.latimes.com/sports/story/2025-02-28/LeBron-james-media-anthony-edwards-face-of-nba-channing-frye.

Skipper, Clay. "Ahmad Rashad Still Has All the Best Michael Jordan Stories." GQ, 7 May 2020, www.gq.com/story/ahmad-rashad-the-last-dance-interview.

Staff, From NBA.com. "Top NBA Finals Moments: John Paxson's 3-Pointer Seals Three-Peat for Bulls", 21 Sept. 2022, www.nba.com/news/history-finals-moments-john-paxson-3-pointer-1993.

Staff, From NBA.com. Top NBA Finals Moments: Steve Kerr's Jumper Sinks Jazz in 1997, NBA.com, 21 Sept. 2022, www.nba.com/news/history-finals-mo

ments-steve-kerr-jumper-1997.

Staff, From NBA.com. "Top NBA Finals Moments: John Paxson's 3-Pointer Seals Three-Peat for Bulls." NBA, NBA.com, 21 Sept. 2022, www.nba.com/news/ history-finals-moments-john-paxson-3-pointer-1993.

Tan, John Jefferson. "The NBA Shortened the Three Point Line to Increase League," Basketball Network, 6 Nov. 2023, www.basketballnetwork.net/old-school/when-the-nba-shortened-the-3-point-line-to-increase-scoring-and-de crease-physicality.

"Teams Defense: Stats." NBA, www.nba.com/stats/teams/ defense?Season=2017-18&SeasonType=Regular+Sea son&dir=-1&sort=DEF_RATING. Accessed 2 Apr. 2025.

Terranova, Justin. "LeBron James Eviscerates Stephen A. Smith on His Own Network as He Breaks Silence on Confrontation." New York Post, New York Post, 26 Mar. 2025, nypost.com/2025/03/26/sports/LeBron-james-breaks-silence-on-stephen-a-smith-confronta tion/.

Thinking Basketball. "Detailed Analysis of LeBron James at His Best | Greatest Peaks Ep. 13." YouTube, YouTube, 1 Mar. 2021, www.youtube.com/watch?v=_ cYVXHi8EJY.

"This Date in NBA History: Steve Kerr's funny parade speech after 1997 NBA Finals." NBA, www.nba.com/watch/ video/this-date-in-nba-history-steve-kerrs-funny-pa rade-speech-after-1997-nba-finals. Accessed 2 Apr. 2025.

Torre, Pablo. "Unmasking the Scorekeeper Who Faked NBA

History." *Pablo Torre Finds Out,* Pablo Torre Finds Out, 27 Feb. 2024, www.pablo.show/p/unmasking-the-scorekeeper-who-faked.

Walder, Chris. "NBA Finals Historical Series Odds List." Odds Shark, 24 Apr. 2024, www.oddsshark.com/nba/nba-finals-historical-series-odds-list.

What's Wright? With Nick Wright. "Michael Jordan's 1987/88 DPOY Stats Fabricated, How Does This Impact His Legacy?" YouTube, YouTube, 20 Jun. 2024. https://youtu.be/V7Gd1sFO2by?si=XKEjjLGsfH6so

Zayas, Pete. "The Different Eras of Kobe Bryant: The Youngest All-Star Starter in NBA History." *The New York Times*, The New York Times, 31 Jan. 2020, www.nytimes.com/athletic/1575802/2020/01/31/the-different-eras-of-kobe-bryant-the-youngest-all-star-starter-in-nba-history

www.ingramcontent.com/pod-product-compliance
Lightning Source LLC
Chambersburg PA
CBHW060349090426
42734CB00011B/2080